Sali zämme
your Baseldütsch survival guide

Sali zämme
your Baseldütsch survival guide

by Sergio J. Lievano & Nicole Egger
Baseldütsch by Walter Loeliger

Illustrations © 2012 Sergio J. Lievano
Watercolour (pages 1 and 17) © 2012 Miguel Lievano

© 2012 Bergli Books

Also available as:
Hoi – your Swiss German survival guide (based on the dialect spoken in Zürich)
Hoi Zäme – Schweizerdeutsch leicht gemacht (for High German speakers)
Hoi! Et après… Manuel de survie en suisse allemand (for French speakers)

Published 2012
Bergli Books   Tel.: +41 61 373 27 77
CH-4001 Basel   Fax: +41 61 373 27 78
Switzerland   E-Mail: info@bergli.ch
                      www.bergli.ch

All rights reserved. No part of this publication may be reproduced, stored in a retrieval system, or transmitted, in any form, or by any means, electronic, mechanical, photocopying, recording or otherwise, without the prior permission in writing from Bergli Books, CH-4001 Basel, Switzerland.

ISBN 978-3-905252-26-2

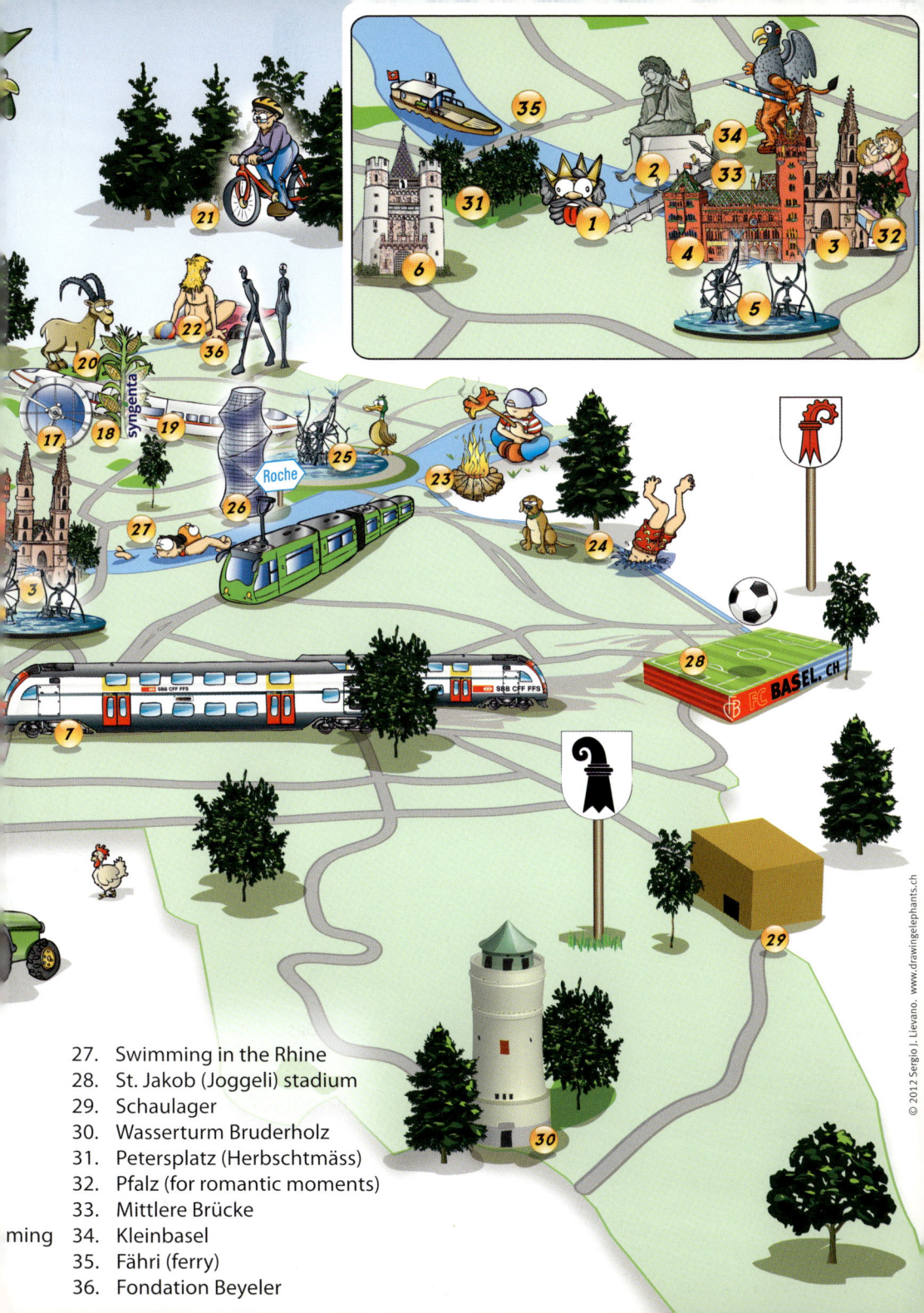

27. Swimming in the Rhine
28. St. Jakob (Joggeli) stadium
29. Schaulager
30. Wasserturm Bruderholz
31. Petersplatz (Herbschtmäss)
32. Pfalz (for romantic moments)
33. Mittlere Brücke
34. Kleinbasel
35. Fähri (ferry)
36. Fondation Beyeler

Sali zämme
your Baseldütsch survival guide

by
Sergio J. Lievano & Nicole Egger

Illustrations and design by
Sergio J. Lievano

Baseldütsch by
Walter Loeliger

Table of Contents

Preface — vii

Part I: About Baseldütsch and Swiss German — 3

Introduction to Swiss German — 4
Brief history of the dialects — 6
The use of High German in Switzerland — 8
High German and Baseldütsch — 9
Use of Swiss German and Baseldütsch — 12
Why the Swiss don't like to speak High German — 15

Part II: Survival Kit — 17

Phonetics — 18
  Consonants — 18
  Vowels — 19

Greetings & Socializing — 20
  Introduction — 20
  Understanding the language — 22
  Questions — 24
  Small talk — 25
  Invitations — 28
  Love — 29
  Things to say at special moments — 33

Work — 34

Communication — 38
  Telephone — 38
  E-mail and SMS — 40
  Post office — 42
  Media (News) — 44

Food & Drinks — 46

Health & Safety — 54
  Health — 54
  Human body — 58
  Emotions — 61
  Emergency — 64
  Police — 65

Shopping — 68
  Shopping in general — 68
  Clothes — 70
  Money and banking — 72

Travelling	**74**
Transportation	74
Directions	78
Hotel	81
Outdoors	83
Entertainment	86
People	**90**
Family	90
Babies	92
Age	93
Housing	**94**
Home	94
Neighbours and agencies	98
Miscellaneous	**102**
Numbers	102
Toilets	104
Education	105
General non-specific terms	106
Colours	107
Animals	108
Time	110
Weather and temperature	114
Part III: Decoding the Basler	**117**
Slang words in Baseldütsch	118
Swiss idioms in Baseldütsch	122
Frequent confusions	126
Appendix	**131**
Pronouns and articles	132
Verbs	134
Dictionary	**137**
English-Baseldütsch	138
Baseldütsch-English	148
Index	**159**
About the authors	**162**
Acknowledgements	**164**

Preface

If you want to feel at home in the region of Basel, nothing will speed the process more than becoming acquainted with Baseldütsch. This book provides valuable tools, both for newcomers and for people who have been struggling with this Swiss dialect for a long time.

Swiss German is not one language, but the name given to a group of very different Alemannic dialects. These dialects (their vocabulary, intonation and pronunciation) vary considerably from one neighbourhood to another. It is a spoken language, and there are contradictory spelling systems for the few occasions when it is written. Although the dialects vary in pronunciation and vocabulary, the Swiss usually understand dialects other than their own. This book will help you to do that, too. Sharing a language that has so many variations keeps Swiss hearts and souls united.

Sali zämme – your Baseldütsch survival guide is based on the modern dialect spoken in Basel and its neighbourhood. Even though Baseldütsch is an oral language, is not standardised, and has many varieties, people from all levels of society in Basel are proud to speak it. Like all Swiss dialects, Baseldütsch has different spelling systems for the few occasions when it is written (see page 18).

Sali zämme - your Baseldütsch survival guide

Introduction to Swiss German

The Swiss German dialects, the languages spoken in the German-speaking part of Switzerland, are different from the German spoken in Germany. The varieties of Swiss German dialects in Switzerland cannot be defined so easily. No particular dialect is considered better than others. Speaking dialect is also not considered 'uneducated' or 'substandard' compared to the written High German but is spoken proudly. A Swiss can identify where another Swiss grew up simply from the dialect spoken. For a Swiss German speaker, language is much more than a way of communication: it is an integral part of his/her national, regional and even personal identity.

About Swiss German

It is said that each Swiss valley had its own dialect. This is not an exaggeration. Mountains and other geographical barriers have enabled some dialects to develop and keep unique expressions. Some dialects, such as the ones spoken in the Swiss Midlands, have intermingled.

Dialäggtgmisch

The interaction of speakers of different dialects has made the peculiarities of some dialects less prevalent. The increasing mobility of the Swiss accelerates this process and leads to a **'Dialäggtgmisch'** – a mixture of different dialects.

Sali zämme - your Baseldütsch survival guide

Brief history of the dialects

Alemannic tribes settled in Switzerland after the fall of the Roman Empire in the 5th century. These tribes lived predominantly along the Rhine and in the central and north-eastern regions. From there Alemannic evolved into three major groups: 'Low', 'High' and 'Highest' Alemannic. These are not qualitative terms in any way. These are the geographical terms describing where the dialect is spoken. The 'Low', located in the Basel area; the 'High', in the vast majority of regions in Switzerland, and the 'Highest' Alemannic, found in the remote area of the Wallis. **Baseldütsch** is now the only dialect based on Low Alemannic.

At the beginning of the 20th century, linguists thought Swiss dialects would disappear by the end of the century and that the standard High German of Germany would prevail in the German-speaking part of Switzerland. But the Swiss German dialects are still going strong and are widespread as a spoken language in practically all situations of daily life.

The radical political events at the beginning of the 20th century and the growth of nationalism helped the Swiss retain their dialects as a form of national identity. During the 1930s many Swiss felt the need to distinguish themselves from the Germans, and speaking their Swiss dialect was a way of expressing Swiss patriotism.

About Swiss German

Nevertheless, in modern Switzerland the use and popularity of Swiss German is steadily increasing.

It continues to gain recognition and popularity, especially among the young, who like hearing it in Swiss popular music or composing written forms of it in their e-mail and SMS messages.

There have been many efforts to agree upon a consolidation of the main dialects into a standard Swiss German that could be written. Rules exist, but the Swiss enjoy their diversity too much to agree on a unified Swiss German. Likewise you will find different spellings of the same **Baseldütsch** word in local newspapers and ads.

The Swiss German code

Although it is not well documented, it has been said on many occasions that throughout history, Swiss German dialects were sometimes used as a 'secret coding system' by people and institutions dealing directly or indirectly in political affairs.

Sali zämme - your Baseldütsch survival guide

The use of High German in Switzerland

Switzerland has what is defined as **'diglossia'**: a situation of a society with two languages closely related and functionally complementary. Swiss German is the spoken language and High German, called **'Schriftdeutsch'** in Switzerland, is the official written language. High German is widely used in the written and spoken media, at schools, and also in official, social, political or religious events where French-speaking Swiss, Italian-speaking Swiss and other non Swiss-German speakers might be present. Swiss German, on the other hand, is spoken in everyday, informal situations, while shopping or socializing with friends and family, in local and regional radio and TV programs, in kindergartens, local government and non-government institutions.

Having diglossia sometimes makes it difficult to know which language is most appropriate to speak – High German or dialect. Since High German is their second language, Swiss German speakers are often reluctant to speak High German which does not always make it easy for them to communicate in it.

About Swiss German

High German and Baseldütsch

Translation: Poor chap! No one told him about 'Baseldütsch'...

The intonation of **Baseldütsch** gives emphasis to the first syllable and pitch is more melodious than in High German. The prime characteristic of most Swiss dialects is the deep-throated, guttural **'ch'**. This is far less prominent in Baseldütsch. For example Baseldütsch uses the same word as the often quoted **Chuchichäschtli** (small kitchen cupboard) but it is pronounced as **Kuchikäschtli**.

In Baseldütsch you use the diminutive in nouns as often as possible by placing the ending '**-li**' onto it. For example **Gipfeli** (croissant), **Drämmli** (tram), **Schätzli** (sweetheart), **Zolli** (zoo), **Kätzli** (little cat), etc.

Sali zämme - your Baseldütsch survival guide

Baseldütsch is also very receptive to the influences of foreign languages, in particular French. Due to its geographical and cultural proximity to France, Baseldütsch has acquired a lot of French vocabulary, as opposed to how foreign words are 'Germanized' in Germany or Austria and most other Swiss dialects. The following table shows some examples of French influences on Baseldütsch:

Baseldütsch	French	High German	English
meersi	merci	danke	thank you
s Welo	le velo	das Fahrrad	bicycle
dr Guafföör	le coiffeur	der Frisör	hairdresser
s Pule	le poulet	das Hähnchen	chicken
s Schminee	la cheminée	der Kamin	fireplace
s Spidaal	l'hôpital	das Krankenhaus	hospital
dr Kondüggtöör	le conducteur	der Schaffner	train conductor
s Lawaboo	le lavabo	das Waschbecken	sink
s Desseer	le dessert	der Nachtisch	dessert
s Drottuaar	le trottoir	der Gehsteig	Footpath/sidewalk
s Guweer	le couvert	der Umschlag	envelope

The four High German cases of nominative, accusative, dative and genitive are reduced in Baseldütsch to only two: First there is the 'common case', which covers the German accusative and the nominative. A Basler (a person from Basel) does not distinguish between them and asks in both cases **Wär** (who): **Wär isch do? Wär hesch gseh?** (Who is here? Whom did you see?). Then there is the 'dative case', which does likewise for the dative and the genitive. (See the Pronouns and articles section page 132.)

About Swiss German

There are certain misconceptions about Swiss dialects, due mainly to the fact that they are spoken rather than written. Some people claim an absence of tenses, a lack of gender and of articles. Baseldütsch certainly has its own particular tenses (see the Verbs Section in the Appendix), but it usually has the same genders as in High German. And it uses articles, even though these, as in most spoken languages, are abbreviated at a conversational level (see table on previous page).

The main differences between Baseldütsch and High German are related to vocabulary and pronunciation (intonation). Baseldütsch keeps its unique, special terms and keeps the original pronunciation of foreign words that are always creeping into the language.

Translation: Hey! Someone stole your bike!

Sali zämme - your Baseldütsch survival guide

Use of Swiss German and Baseldütsch

The Swiss German language group is the largest in Switzerland. According to Swiss statistics, *63.7% of the Swiss population speak this language in their daily lives, followed by French with 20.4 %, Italian with 6.5%, and Romansch (a language with four dialects that was officially recognized only in the 1930s) with 0.5% or 35,000 people.

The diversity of languages and their uneven distribution generate political and social discussions. The '**Röschtigraben**' (fried–potato trench) is the name given to the ideological and linguistic border between the Swiss German and the French-speaking area. It is not that there is any real conflict on this imaginary border. The relationship between neighbours is cordial and there is no hate or bitterness (other than the occasional reciprocal jokes). The Röschtigraben term – a kind of potato tortilla that originated in the German-speaking part of Switzerland – denotes a different mind set between the two language groups, which is usually highlighted in the political arena.

In this case the Baslers are non-conformists. In terms of language, Basel is certainly part of German-speaking Switzerland but in terms of culture and political decisions, Basel votes and thinks similar to French-speaking Switzerland. You could say it belongs on the other side of the Röschtigraben.

* from press release 0351-0213-10 of the Swiss Federal Statistical Office, December 19, 2002.

About Swiss German

The Swiss spare no effort to smooth out differences whenever possible and to equalize distribution of power and influence. The federalist form of government helps people living in Switzerland to maintain and respect regional and local distinctions.

Other languages are : *

Spanish	1.1 %
Serbian and Croatian	1.4 %
Portuguese	1.2 %
Turkish	0.6 %
English	1.0 %
Albanian	1.3 %
Other languages	2.4 %

The large number of non-Swiss plays an important role in the development of Swiss German. New Swiss generations come not only from Swiss families, but from a mixture of different nationalities and cultural backgrounds. These children of immigrants are called '**Secondos**'. They may have little or no identity with their parents' original country and yet they may not be considered Swiss either.

Sali zämme - your Baseldütsch survival guide

The 'Secondos'...
a term that implies the second generation – act as a bridge of communication between their older relatives and Swiss people and add many new flavours to Swiss German.

Global influences
Young Swiss are of course also influenced by foreign music, foreign fashion, travel and the media, and are always adding new expressions to Swiss German. Like in other countries, Swiss youngsters create their own language identities, separating themselves from older generations.

About Swiss German

Why the Swiss don't like to speak High German

ALL I DID WAS ASK IF HE COULD SPEAK HIGH GERMAN...

Many foreigners who learn to speak High German complain that Swiss people only reluctantly reply in High German. Apparently Swiss people generally don't like to speak High German. Why is that so?

For the Swiss, High German is a foreign language. The Swiss prefer to speak their Swiss dialect even though High German is the official German language in Switzerland. High German is the language of school and the language of rules and regulations, but it is rarely associated with pleasure and leisure. On top of this, High German is even for school teachers a foreign language, meaning that they, too, speak a 'helvetic' kind of High German. A lot of Swiss people lack confidence in speaking High German and feel awkward using it.

Although the size and economic power of Germany may sometimes seem threatening to them, a lot of Swiss people are reluctant to speak High German because they feel language-wise in an inferior position rather than because of any animosity towards Germany.

For Swiss people it is particularly unpleasant to speak High German in the company of other Swiss. First they think of this as 'putting on airs' and second they fear making a fool of themselves in front of other Swiss.

Sali zämme - your Baseldütsch survival guide

Consonants

TIP... Since Baseldütsch is mainly an oral language, one writes it as close to the pronunciation as possible. That's why Baseldütsch uses doubled vowels instead of the High German h or ie to stretch a vowel (**Zaan** instead of **Zahn**, **froo** instead of **froh**, **viil** instead of **viel**). Read the words out loud. A native Baseldütsch speaker also has to do this, because he is not used to reading his own dialect.

 Phonetics of Swiss German are one of the most complex subjects to discuss. This book gives an approximation of the standard way modern Baseldütsch is pronounced today. You will find people who will say that they would pronounce or write certain words differently.

Phonetics: Consonants

b	as in **B**lues	ng	as in si**ng**
ch	as in Lo**ch** Ness or Ba**ch**, always voiceless at the back of the throat	ngg	as in bli**nk**
		p	as in **P**izza
		qu	as in **Qu**antity
d	as in **D**oor	r	as in Bu**rr**ito
f	as in **F**inger	s	as in **s**ad (voiceless)
g	as in **G**od	sp and schp	the s or sch before a p as in **sh**e
gg	short strong k as in **K**ing	st and scht	the s or sch before a t as in **sh**e
gw	as in **Qu**est	t	as in **T**able
h	as in **H**ip-**H**op	tz	zz as in Pi**zz**a.
k	aspirated kh as in **K**ilo	v	as in **F**inger
l	as in **L**ion	w	as in **V**alentine
m	as in **M**e	x	as in **X**enophobe
n	as in **N**ight	z	as in **Z**ombie

Survival Kit

Vowels

Phonetics: vowels

a, aa	as in **a**rm or as in f**a**ther	**ie**	as in r**e**al
ä, ää	as in c**a**t or as in f**a**mily	**o, oo**	as in **o**ff or as in d**oo**r
äi, ääi	as in f**i**re or as in **i**pod	**ö, öö**	as in w**o**rry or as the 'u' in b**u**rn
au	as in **ou**t	**u, uu**	as in f**u**ll or as in c**oo**l
e, ee	as in b**e**t or as in b**e**nd	**ü, üü**	as in French T**u**
ei	as in M**ay**	**üe**	as a variation of ie (as in r**e**al). Exists in Baseldütsch, but is in the dictionary written as ie
i, ii	as in **I**taly or as in **ea**gle		
j	as in **y**ellow		

BE AWARE... Every word is written as a single word, even if consisting of only one letter (**Das isch z grooss** = that's too big).

Words having strong consonants in High German, usually have weak consonants in Baseldütsch (**Blatz** = place, **Boscht** = post). But the 'tz' used in High German is being kept in Baseldütsch, even though pronounced as a sharp (doubled) z (**glotze** = to stare)

BE AWARE... In traditional Baseldütsch you sometimes distinguish between **i/ii** (an open i as kling) and **y/yy** (closed as seen). In this book and in most modern dialect dictionaries this distinction is not made. Even many people in Basel cannot tell the difference. You will, however, still see the y used in Basel, especially during Fasnacht (carnival).

BE AWARE... Rememeber: In written Baseldütsch the letter 'w' is pronounced as in 'very' and not as in 'wary'. E.g. **Welo (n)** (franz.: vélo) = Bicycle

When a word ending with a vowel is followed by one beginning with a vowel, the letter 'n' is added to the preceding word. E.g. **Schönen Oobe!** (have a nice evening)

* LÄÄDELE : TO GO SHOPPING.

Sali zämme – your Baseldütsch survival guide

Introduction

Greetings & Socializing

Formal and informal

Baseldütsch (as High German) differentiates between the formal and the informal way of approaching a person. The formal way uses the pronoun **Sii** and the person is usually addressed by his/her last name (Good morning Mr. Meier), the informal way is used with the pronoun **du** and the person can be addressed by his/her first name (Hi Chris…).

Saying hello (formal)

Good morning Mr. / Mrs. …	Guete Moorge Herr / Frau …
	Guete Daag
Good afternoon	Guete Nomidaag
Good evening	Gueten Oobe
Hello	Griezi
Hello (to several people)	Griezi mitenander
How are you?	Wie goots Iine?
Fine, and you?	Guet, und Iine?
Pleased to meet you	Freut mi Sii kenne z leere.
'Bye	Uff Wiiderluege
	Uff Wiidersee
	Adiöö *(franz.: adieu)*

Formal (Sii)

To be used in business, with strangers, or whenever you meet adults who haven't introduced themselves with their first names. Usually the older, more senior person offers the '**du**' form (**Sii könne du zu mir saage** or, **Wämmer Duzis mache?**)

Survival Kit

BE AWARE... In this book the abbreviation (inf) is used for informal and (fr) is used for formal. For nouns: (m) is masculine, (f) is feminine, (n) is neutral and (pl) is plural.

Greetings & Socializing

Saying hello (informal)

Hi	Sali / Salli
Hi (to several people)	Sali zämme / Salli zämme
How are you?	Wie goots?
Fine, and you?	Guet, und dir?
Quite OK.	S goot eso.
I am not so well.	Mir goots nit so guet.
'Bye.	Tschau / Tschüss
See you.	Me seet sich.
Pleased to meet you.	Fröit mi dii kenne z leere.
See you later.	Bis spööter.
Have a nice day / evening.	Schööne Daag / Schöönen Oobe.

WARNING !

Informal: (du / diir)

Usually used with children, friends, family, and among students and colleagues, not with someone of authority.

Sali zämme - your Baseldütsch survival guide

Understanding the language

Key survival phrases

Do you speak English?	Könne Sii Änglisch? (fr)
	Kasch (du) Änglisch? (inf)
Sorry, I don't understand.	Entschuldigung, ich verstand Sii nit. (fr)
	Entschuldigung, ich verstand dii nit. (inf)
What did you say?	Was hänn Sii gsäit? (fr)
	Was hesch (du) gsäit? (inf)
Can you repeat what you said?	Könne Sii das bitte nomoll wiiderhoole? (fr)
	Kasch (du) das bitte nomoll wiiderhoole? (inf)
Could you write it down?	Könnte Sii mir das bitte uffschriibe? (fr)
	Kasch (du) mir das bitte uffschriibe? (inf)
Can you say it again slowly?	Könne Sii das bitte nomoll langsam saage? (fr)
	Kasch (du) das bitte nomoll langsam saage? (inf)
I don't speak Swiss German.	Ich kaa nit Schwizerdütsch.

TIP... **Könne** is used for both ability and politeness (are you able to? / could you?). In the formal question, the form is **Könne Sii**?; the informal question is **Kasch (du)**?. For verb conjugation in Baseldütsch check the table on page 134.

Survival Kit

Being polite

In Switzerland (as in many other countries) a golden rule for good communication and understanding is to be polite. Therefore the following words may be very useful when meeting people:

please	Bitte.
thank you	Dangge / Meersi *(franz.: merci)*
thanks a lot	Dangge viilmool.
excuse me	Entschuldigung / Exgüüsi *(franz.: excusez)*
May I ...?	Könnt ich bitte ...?
	Daarf ich bitte ...?
yes, please	Joo, bitte.
no, thank you	Näi, dangge.
I am sorry.	S duet mer läid.
You are welcome.	Bitte, gärn gschee.
You are very kind.	Sii sind schampaar nätt. (fr)
	Sii sind schampaar hilfsberäit. (fr)
	Du bisch schampaar nätt. (inf)
	Du bisch schampaar hilfsberäit. (inf)
Would you mind ...?	Könnte Sii bitte ...? (fr)
	Könntsch (du) bitte ...? (inf)

Greetings & Socializing

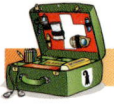

Sali zämme - your Baseldütsch survival guide

Questions

TIP... 1. For open questions, where the potential answers are unlimited, the question always starts with a question word (also called w-word) **Woo woonsch?** (Where do you live?), **Waas isch di Lieblingsmuusig?** (What's your favourite music?)

2. For closed questions, where the answer is either yes or no, there is no special question word. The question starts with a verb and then the subject: **Kaasch** (du) **Dütsch**? (Do you speak German?) **Schaffsch** (du) **in Basel**? (Do you work in Basel?)

Why?
Werum?

When?
Wenn?

How?
Wie?

Where?
Woo?

How many?
Wie viil?

Who with?
Mit wäm?

How long?
Wie lang?

From where?
Vo woo?

To where.?
Wo aane?

How much?
Wie viil?

What?
Waas?

Who?
Wäär?

What for?
Werum?/ Für waas?

Survival Kit

Small talk

Greetings & Socializing

Introducing yourself

What is your name?	Wie isch Iire Naame? (fr)
	Wie häisse Sii? (fr)
	Wie isch di Naame? (inf)
	Wie häissisch (du)? (inf)
My name is …	Ich häiss …
Where are you from?	Vo woo kömme Sii? (fr)
	Vo woo kunnsch (du)? (inf)
I come from …	Ich kumm uss …
Where do you live?	Wo woone Sii? (fr)
	Wo woonsch (du)? (inf)
I live in …	Ich woon in …
How long have you been here?	Wie lang sinn Sii scho doo? (fr)
	Wie lang bisch (du) scho doo? (inf)
I have been here for … years.	Ich bi scho … Joor doo.
What do you do in your spare time?	Was mache Sii in Iirer Freizit? (fr)
	Was machsch (du) in diiner Freizit? (inf)
I like … / I love …	Ich ha … gäärn / Ich due gäärn …
I'm interested in …	Ich interessier mi für …

TIP… In written short texts the subject of the first person singular or plural can be left out. Example: **Bii in zää Minute wiider doo.** or: **Göön hütt zoobe ins Kino.**

Sali zämme - your Baseldütsch survival guide

 The German word **ledig** means not married. The English word **single** is also used in Baseldütsch, but it only means with no boyfriend / girlfriend (not in a relationship). So one can be **ledig** but not **single**, meaning one lives with somebody without being married.

Getting personal

Are you married?	Sinn Sii ghüüroote? (fr)
	Sinn Sii verhüürootet (fr)
	Bisch (du) ghüüroote? (inf)
	Bisch (du) verhüürootet? (inf)
Are you single?	Sinn Sii singel? (fr)
	Bisch (du) singel? (inf)
Do you have a boy / girlfriend?	Hänn Sii e Fründ / e Fründin? (fr)
	Hesch (du) e Fründ / e Fründin? (inf)
Do you have children?	Hänn Sii Kinder? (fr)
	Hesch (du) Kinder? (inf)
How is your family?	Wie goots Iirer Familie? (fr)
	Wie goots diner Familie? (inf)
What's your telephone number?	Wie isch Iiri Delifonnummere? (fr)
	Wie isch di Delifonnummere? (inf)
My number is …	Mi Nummere isch …
I don't have an e-mail address.	Ich ha käi Ii-Meil-Adrässe.
What's your address?	Wie isch Iiri Adrässe? (fr)
	Wie isch di Adrässe? (inf)
Which street?	An weelere Stroose?

Survival Kit

Greetings & Socializing

First approach

Do you want to go and have a drink?	Wänn Sii äins / äine go zie? (fr)
	Wänn Sii öppis go dringge? (fr)
	Wotsch äins / äine go zie? (inf)
	Wotsch öppis go dringge? (inf)
Can I invite you for a drink?	Daarf ich line e Drink spendiere? (fr)
	Daarf ich dir e Drink spendiere? (inf)
Do you want to come with me / us ?	Kunnsch (du) mit miir / uns?
Are you coming?	Kömme Sii? (fr) / Kunnsch? (inf)
Let's go somewhere.	Kumm, mer göön nöime aane.
Do I know you from somewhere?	Kenn ich Sii vo nöime?(fr) / Kenne mir uns?
	Kenn ich dii vo nöime? (inf)
Do you want to dance?	Wänn Sii go danze?(fr)
	Wotsch (du) danze? (inf)
Do you have a cigarette?	Hätte Sii mir e Zigerette? (fr)
	Hesch mer e Zigerette? (inf)

Negative answers

No, I don't smoke.	Näi, i rauch nit.
I have to go now.	Ich muess jetz goo.
Please, leave me alone!	Löön Sii mii bitte in Rue! (fr)
	Loss mii bitte in Rue! (inf)
Get lost!	Hau ab! (inf) / Haue Sii ab! (fr)
I have to work tomorrow.	Ich muess moorn schaffe.
I don't think so.	Ich glaub nit.
I want to go home.	Ich möcht häi.
I need to go home.	Ich muess häi.
I have no time.	Ich ha käi Ziit.
I don't have any money.	Ich ha käi Gäld.
I don't feel like it.	Ich ha käi Luscht.

 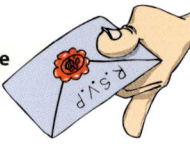

Sali zämme - your Baseldütsch survival guide

Invitations

Key survival phrases

English	Baseldütsch
May I invite you for dinner tomorrow night?	Darf ich Sii moorn zoobe zem Äsre iilaade?(fr) / Darf ich dii moorn zoobe zem Äsre iilaade?(inf)
Yes, I would love to come.	Joo, ich kumm gärn.
Thank you for the invitation.	Dangge für d Iilaadig.
to be on time	pünggtlig sii
to be late	verspöötet sii, z spoot koo
Sorry for being late.	Endschuldigung für d Verspöötig.
The food is delicious.	S Äsre isch seer fein. / S Äsre schmeggt wunderbaar.
Please bring your partner.	Sii könne gäärn Ire Paartner / Iiri Paartnere mitnää. (fr) / Du kasch gäärn di Fründ / di Fründin mitnää. (inf)
No, I am sorry, but I have another appointment.	Duet mer läid, denn kaan i nit. Ich haa denn scho öppis anders voor.

TIP... People usually bring something to a party. The most common gifts are wine, sweets or flowers. When invited to a barbecue or an informal party, it is polite to offer to bring some food: **Kaan i öppis mitbringe?** (Can I bring something?)

Common events

English	Baseldütsch
Barbecue	Grillfescht (n)
Birthday party	Gebuurtstaagspaarti (f)
Brunch	Bröntsch (m)
Coffee party	Kaffiklatsch (m) / Kaffikränzli (n)
Dinner	Znacht (m) / Znachtässe (n)
Farewell party	Abschiidsfescht (n)
Hen night / Stag night	Bolteroobe (m)
Housewarming party	Huusiiweiigspaarti (f)
Lunch	Zmittagässe (n)
Party	Fescht (n) / Paarti (f)

Greetings & Socializing

Survival Kit

Love

TIP... The Swiss and the Basler are keen on pet names, the most common ones are:

Schätzli	little treasure
Tübli	little dove
Müüsli	little mouse
Kääferli	little beetle
Schnuggi / Schnüggerli	sweetie
Bäärli	little bear

Greetings & Socializing

Key survival phrases

to love	gäärn haa / liebe
I love you.	Ich ha dii gäärn.
I need you.	Ich bruuch dii.
I miss you.	Ich vermiss dii.
You are very pretty / sexy.	Du bisch seer hübsch / sexi.
You are the love of my life.	Du bisch d Liebi vo mim Lääbe.
Kiss me.	Küss mii.
I've fallen in love with you.	Ich haa mi in dii verliebt.
We fell in love.	Mir hänn uns verliebt.
I am in love.	Ich bi verliebt.
Let's move in / live together.	Kumm, mir zien zämme.
You make me very happy.	Du machsch mi totaal glügglig.
She is my girlfriend.	Sii isch mi Fründin.
He is my boyfriend.	Äär isch mi Fründ.
We are just friends.	Mir sinn nuur Kolleege.
We love each other.	Mir hänn uns gärn.
I like her / him.	Äär / Sii gfallt miir.
Love at first sight.	Liebi uf en erschte Bligg.
We first met in ...	Mir hänn uns in … kenne gleert.
Partner	Paartner (m) / Paartnere (f)
	Lääbespaartner (m) / Lääbespaartnere (f)
to get to know each other	sich kenne leere

Sali zämme - your Baseldütsch survival guide

BE AWARE... In Baseldütsch the words **Fründ (m)** and **Fründin (f)** refer to a friend, as well as a boyfriend or girlfriend.
When you want to make it clear that somebody is your boyfriend or girlfriend, you may say: **mi Fründ** (my friend) for boyfriend or **mi Fründin** for girlfriend. **E Fründ (m)** or **e Fründin (f)**, on the other hand, is just a friend.
The word **Kolleeg** is also used for friends, including friends outside work that aren't colleagues in the English sense.

WARNING !

Many misunderstandings are made just by the wrong usage of the preposition that comes together with the verb. In order not to jeopardise good communication keep in mind the following:

Sleep at John's / Anna's place
bim John/ bi der Anna schloofe
Sleep next to John / Anna
nääben em John/ nääbe der Anna schloofe
Sleep with John/ Anna (to have sex).
mit em John/ mit der Anna schloofe

Sexual preferences

I like women.	Ich stand uf Fraue.
I like men.	Ich stand uf Männer.
heterosexual	hetero(sexuell)
homosexual	homo(sexuell)
gay	schwuul
lesbian	lesbisch

Survival Kit

Wedding stuff

to get engaged	sich verloobe
I got engaged.	Ich ha mi verlobt.
to get married	hüüroote
to be married	ghüüroote sii
I am married.	Ich bi ghüüroote.
Marriage	Ee (f)
Wedding	Hochzit (f)
We are getting married.	Mir hüüroote.
Stag / hen party	Bolteroobe (m)
Do you want to marry me?	Möchtsch duu mi hüüroote? (inf)
	Möchtsch duu mi Frau / mi Maa wärde? (inf)
Yes, I do.	Joo, ich will.
No, I don't want to / yet.	Näi, ich möcht nit / noonig.

Greetings & Socializing

GRAMMAR

Sich verloobe / sich verliebe are reflexive verbs. Reflexive verbs have the following conjugation:

ich verlieb mi
du verliebsch di
är/sii verliebt sich
mir verliebe uns
dir verliebet öich
sii verliebe sich

Sali zämme - your Baseldütsch survival guide

Greetings & Socializing

Loveless (informal)

English	Baseldütsch
I don't want to see you again.	Ich möcht dii nie mee gsee.
There is someone else.	Ich haa en andere (m) / en anderi. (f)
I hate you.	Ich hass dii.
Let's take a break.	Kumm, mir machen e Pause.
Have you been unfaithful?	Hesch du mi bedrooge?
We are just friends.	Mir sinn nur Kolleege.
I am not in love.	Ich bi nit verliebt.
to move out	uuszie
S/he moved out.	Sii/Äär isch usszooge.
to have an affair	en Affääre haa
to betray somebody	öpper bedriege / bschisse
S/he betrayed me.	Sii/Äär het mii bedrooge.
Argument	Lämpe (plur.) / Buff (n) / Händel (m) / Striit (m)
argue	händle / kääre / stritte
to separate	sich drenne
to get a divorce	sich schäide loo
divorced	gschiide
to hate each other	sich hasse

GRAMMAR

Sich schäide loo is an expression that is used in the following way:

Ich loo mii schäide.
(I am getting a divorce)
Ich will mii schäide loo.
(I want to get a divorce)
Sii löön sich schäide.
(They are getting a divorce)

HELVI...DARLING!
I ONLY SAID THAT SHOPPING SEEMS CHEAPER ON THE OTHER SIDE OF THE BORDER...

Survival Kit

Things to say at special moments

Greetings & Socializing

Survival words and phrases

Beautiful!	Schöön!
Best wishes!	Alles Gueti!
Break a leg!	Hals- und Bäibruch!
Cheers!	Broscht! / Gsundhäit! / Zem Wool! / Santee! (franz.: Santé)
Congratulations!	Alles Gueti! Gratulazioon!
Delicious!	Heerlig!
Enjoy your meal!	E Guete!
Fantastic!	Fantastisch!
Get well!	Gueti Besserig!
Good Luck!	Viil Glügg! / Viil Erfolg!
Happy Anniversary!	Alles Gueti zum Jubilääum!
Happy Birthday!	Alles Gueti zum Gebuurtsdaag!
Happy New Year!	Alles Gueti fürs nöie Joor! E guets Nöis! / E guete Rutsch!
Have a nice trip!	Schööni Räis!
I wish you success!	Viil Erfolg!
I wish you…	Ich wünsch dir (inf) / Iine (fr) …
Merry Christmas!	Schööni Wienacht!
To your health!	Uff di Gsundhäit!
Welcome!	Willkomme!

Misfortune and sympathy

Sorry.	Ojee. / Das duet mer läid.
My deepest condolences.	Mi Biiläid. / Das duet mer läid.
I hope you get well soon.	I hoff s goot bald besser.
Tough luck	Bäch
Better luck next time.	Viil Glück s näggscht Mool.
What a shame!	Schaad!
I warned you.	I haa di gwaarnt.

Sali zämme - your Baseldütsch survival guide

Work

Key survival phrases

Do you work?	Sinn Sii bruefsdäätig? / Schaffe Sii? (fr)
	Bisch (du) bruefsdäätig? / Schaffsch (du)? (inf)
What do you do?	Was mache Sii? / Was schaffe Sii? (fr)
	Was machsch (du)? / Was schaffsch (du)? (inf)
What is your profession?	Was sinn Sii vo Bruef ? (fr)
	Was hänn Sii gleert? (fr)
	Was bisch (du) vo Bruef ? (inf)
	Was hesch (du) gleert? (inf)
I am...	Ich bi ...
Where do you work?	Wo schaffe Sii? (fr)
	Wo schaffsch (du)? (inf)
I work at...	Ich schaff bi ...
I work at home.	Ich schaff dehäim.
I work freelance.	Ich bi äigeständig. / Ich schaff als Freelancer.
I am not working.	Ich schaff nit.
I am employed at...	Ich bi ... aagschtellt bi ...
I am unemployed.	Ich bi aarbetsloos. / Ich gang go stämple.
I am self-employed.	Ich bi sälbständig.

Paperwork

Appraisal	Qualifikazioon (f)
	Läischtigsbewäärtig (f)
Contract	Verdraag (m)
Form	Formulaar (n)
Invoice	Rächnig (f)
Job application	Bewäärbig (f)
Minutes	Brotokoll (n)
Plan	Blaan (m)
Purchase order	Bstellig (f)
	Uffdraag (m)
Report	Bricht (m)

Survival Kit

Work

TIP... The working environment in Switzerland is probably the most common place where English and Swiss German merge. English is the international business language, so business terms tend to be in English (e.g. **Customer Service, Finance, Procurement, Supply Chain, HR**…).

Key survival phrases

We have a meeting.	Mir hänn e Sitzig / e Besprächig.
We have a problem.	Mir hänn e Brobleem.
We are successful.	Mir sinn seer erfolgriich.
We made … profit.	Mir hänn … Gwinn gmacht.
We made … turnover.	Mir hänn … Umsatz gmacht.
We made… loss.	Mir hänn … Verluscht gmacht.
We create jobs.	Mir schaffen Aarbetsblätz.
You have the job.	Sii griege die Stell.
You are fired.	Sii sinn entloo.
I want to resign.	Ich möcht künde.
I want a salary raise.	Ich möcht e Loonerhööchig.
Would you have lunch with me?	Kömme Sii mit mir go zmittagässe? (fr)
	Kunnsch (du) mit mir go zmittagässe? (inf)
Could you explain please?	Könne Sii mir das bitte erklääre? (fr)
	Kasch du mir das bitte erklääre? (inf)
I want to go on holiday from …till…	Ich möcht Feerie vom … bis zum ….
Could you make a presentation for me?	Könne Sii mir bitte e Presentazioon mache? (fr)
	Kasch (du) mir bitte e Presentazioon mache? (inf)
I would like to discuss something with you.	Ich möcht öppis mit Iine bespräche. (fr)
	Ich möcht öppis mit dir bespräche. (inf)

Sali zämme - your Baseldütsch survival guide

Work

Time at work

Appointment	Termiin (m)
Break	Pause (f)
Coffee break	Kaffipause (f)
Conference	Komferänz (f)
Course	Kuurs (m)
Job interview	Bewäärbigsgsprööch (n)
Lunch break	Mittagspause (f)
Meeting	Besprächig (f)
	Sitzig (f)
Presentation	Presentazioon (f)
Vacations	Feerie (pl)

Payment

Bonus	Boonus (m)
Commission	Komissioon (f)
Costs	Koschte (pl)
Discounts	Verbilligung (f)
Fee	Gebüür (f)
	Briis (m)
Full time	Vollziit
Insurance	Versicherig (f)
Overtime	Üüberstunde (pl)
Part time	Däilzit
Payment	Zaalig (f)
Pension fund	Bangsioonskasse (f)
Salary	Loon (m)
	Saläär (n)
Taxes	Stüüre (pl)

Working areas

Canteen	Kantiine (f)
	Mensa (f)
Garage	Garaasch (f) / Iistellhalle (f)
Laboratory	Laboor (n)
Office	Gschäft (n)
	Büüro (n)
Parking area	Paarkblatz (m)
Reception	Empfang (m)
Smoking area	Raucheregge (m) /
	Fümuar (n) *(franz.: fumoir)*
Studio	Stuudio (n)
Warehouse	Laagerhalle (f)
Department store	Waarehuus (n)

Dress code

Briefcase	Aarbetsmappe (f)
Business casual	unzwunge
Dress	Gläid (n) / Aazuug (m)
Dress Code	Gläidervoorschrift (f) /
	Gläiderknigge (f)
Suit	Aazuug (m)
Tie	Grawatte (f)
Uniform	Unifoorm (f)

Survival Kit

Work

Job title

Apprentice	Leerling (m)		Mänätschere (f)
Assistant	Assischtänt (m)	**Occupation**	Tschob (m)
	Assischtäntin (f)		Bruef (m)
Board of Directors	Verwaltigsroot (m)	**Owner**	Bsitzer (m)
Boss	Scheff (m) *(franz.: chef)*		Bsitzere (f)
	Scheffin (f)	**Partner**	Paartner (m)
Cleaner	Butzmaa (m)		Paartnere (f)
	Butzfrau (f)	**Professional**	Profi (m/f)
Colleague	Aarbetskolleeg (m)	**Receptionist**	Ressepzionischt (m)
	Aarbetskolleegin (f)		Ressepzionischtin (f)
Consultant	Berooter (m/f)	**Salesperson**	Verköiffer (m)
Customer	Kund (m)		Verköiffere (f)
	Kundin (f)	**Secretary**	Seggredäär (m)
Director	Diräggder (m)		Seggredäärin (f)
	Diräggdere (f)	**Technician**	Techniker (m)
	Diräggdoorin (f)		Technikere (f)
Employee	Aagstellte (m)	**Trainee**	Praktikant (m)
	Aagstellti (f)		Praktikantin (f)
Employer	Aarbetgääber (m)	**Worker**	Aarbäiter / Biezer (m)
	Aarbetgääbere (f)		Aarbäitere / Biezere (f)
Job description	Pflichteheft (n)		
Manager	Mänätscher (m)		

Sali zämme - your Baseldütsch survival guide

Telephone

When calling

May I talk to Mr. X / Ms. Y?	Kann ich bitte mit em Herr X / dr Frau Y reede? (fr)
Could you connect me to Mr. X?	Könnte Sii mi bitte mit em Herr X verbinde? (fr)
I'll connect you.	Ich due Sii verbinde.
Can I call you back?	Kaan ich Iine zrugglütte? (fr)
	Kaan ich dir zrugglütte? (inf)
What are you calling about...?	Um waas goots?

...YOUR CALL IS BEING HELD IN A QUEUE. THE WAITING TIME IS CURRENTLY 25 MINUTES. IN THE MEANTIME, LET US INTRODUCE YOU TO OUR NEW PRODUCTS AND SERVICES THAT WILL ENSURE TOTAL CUSTOMER SATISFACTION...

Telephone words

Answering machine	Delifonbeantworter (m)
Area code	Vorwaal (f)
cancel	lösche
Long distance call	Delifon us em Ussland / ins Ussland
Mobile phone	Händi (n) / Natel (n)
Phone call	Fungg (m) / Delifon (n) / Aaruef (m)
Public telephone	Delifonkabiine (n)
Telephone bill	Delifonrächnig (f)
Telephone book	Delifonbuech (n)
Telephone card	Delifonkaarte (f)
to telephone / call	aalütte / e Fungg gää

Survival Kit

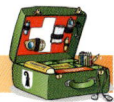

TIP... When answering a phone call, people usually say their full name: Petra Müller. When calling, people usually introduce themselves: **Doo isch d Petra Müller. Könnt ich bitte mit em Herr Meier reede?** (This is Petra Müller speaking. May I talk to Mr. Meier?) A phone conversation is usually ended with: **Uff Wiiderhööre.**

It is also polite to ask **Stöör ich?** (Am I disturbing you?) when calling somebody unexpectedly, or **Hänn Sii e Momänt Zit? (fr)** (Do you have a moment?) at the beginning of a conversation.

Key survival phrases

Can I use your phone?	Kaan ich Iir Delifon bruuche/benutze? (fr)
	Kaan ich di Delifon bruuche/benutze? (inf)
I will call you.	Ich lütt Iine denn aa. (fr)
	Ich lütt dir denn aa. / Ich gib dir e Fungg. (inf)
There was no answer.	S het niemer abgnoo.
The line is busy / engaged.	S isch bsetzt.
I need to recharge my mobile phone.	Ich muess mi Händi / Natel ufflaade.
There is no telephone line.	S isch käi Verbindig. / S kunnt käi Summdoon.
The phone is ringing.	S Delifon lüttet.
Wrong number.	Falsch verbunde.
How much does a minute cost to...?	Wie viil koschtet e Minute uf ...?
Please turn off your mobile phone.	Stelle Sii bitte Iir Händi / Natel ab. (fr)
	Stell bitte di Händi / Natel ab. (inf)

Sali zämme - your Baseldütsch survival guide

E-mail and SMS

Communication

E-Mail

Address book	Adrässbuech (n)
Attachment	Aahang (m) / Aalaag (f) / Biilaag (f) / aaghängti Datei (f)
Connection	Verbindig (f)
copy	kopiere
Desktop	Aarbetsflechi / Schriibtisch (m)
E-mail	Ii-Meil (n) Meil (n)
forward	witerläite
Laptop	Läptop (m)
log in	iilogge / aamälde
log out	usslogge / abmälde
reply	antworte zruggschriibe
Subject	Bedräff (m)
Symbol '@'	Ät / Affeschwanz (m)
Text message	SMS (n)
Trash	Bapiirkoorb (m) Abfall (m)

Key computer terms

burn a CD	e Zeedee (CD) brenne
download	aabelaade
print	drugge
Printer	Drugger (m)
open a new folder	e nöie Ordner aaleege
open a program	e Brogramm uffmache / öffne
save a document	e Dokumänt abschpäichere
Screen	Bildschiirm (m)
turn on the computer	der Compiuuter aastelle
turn off the computer	der Compiuuter abstelle / ussschalte

Survival Kit

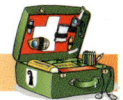

Survival e-mail phrases

I need to check my e-mails.	Ich muess emoll mini Meils aaluege.
There is no internet connection.	S het käi Internetaaschluss.
That is a virus / spam.	Das isch e Viirus / Späm.
I will e-mail you.	Ich schriib Iine e Meil. (fr)
	Ich due dir meile. (inf)
Send me an e-mail.	Schigg mer e Meil. (fr)
	Schigge Sii mir e Meil. (inf)
I deleted your e-mail.	Ich haa Iir Meil glöscht. (fr)
	Ich haa di Meil glöscht. (inf)
Stop sending me e-mails.	Schriibe Sii mir käini Meils me. (fr)
	Schriib mir käini Meils me. (inf)
What's your e-mail?	Wie isch Iiri Meil-Adrässe? (fr)
	Wie isch di Meil-Adrässe? (inf)

Communication

Swiss SMS terms

LG	Liebi Griess (kind regards)
HDG	Haa di gäärn (I love you)
GN8	Guet Nacht (Good night)
8UNG	Achtung / Heb Soorg (be careful / watch out)
CUL8r	See you later
4U	For you

HI!... I WOULD LIKE TO BE YOUR ´FRIEND´...

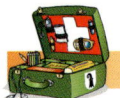

Sali zämme - your Baseldütsch survival guide

Post office

The Post

Address	Adrässe (f)	**Postal money order**	Gäldüüberwiisig (f)
Airmail	Luftboscht (f)	**Postcard**	Boschtkaarte (f)
Attn.	zuhande vo	**Postal code**	Boschtläitzaal (f)
Envelope	Guweer (n) *(franz.: Couvert)*	**Postman**	Böschtler / Briefdrääger (m)
Letter	Brief (m)		Böschtlere / Briefdräägere (f)
Mailbox	Briefkaschte (m)	**Registered letter**	iigschriibene Brief (m)
Packet	Päckli (n)	**Registered mail**	iigschriibeni Boscht (f)
Post	Boscht (f)	**Sender's address**	Absänder/e (m/f)
Post office	Boscht (f)	**Stamp**	Maargge / Briefmaargge (f)
Postage stamp	Boschtstämpel (m)	**to send**	schigge

Survival Kit

Key survival phrases

I'd like to send this letter by priority mail.
Ich möcht dä Brief mit A-Boscht schigge.

I would like to redirect my mail.
Ich möcht mi Boscht umläite.

What's the postal code of …?
Was isch d Boschtläitzaal vo …?

How much does it cost to send this package special delivery?
Wie viil koschtet dä Brief per Express?

How can I apply for a P.O. Box?
Wie kumm ich zum ene Boschtfach?

What's the fastest way to send this letter / package?
Wie kaan ich dä Brief / das Päggli am schnällschte schigge?

What's the cheapest way to send this letter / package?
Wie kaan ich dä Brief / das Päggli am billigschte schigge?

When will it arrive?
Wenn kunnt das aa?

Can you give me a price list?
Hätte Sii mir e Priislischte?

TIP… The Swiss postal system offers different possibilities for sending letters and packages. The most common ones are:

B-Boscht: Low priority delivery. Within Switzerland it usually takes two to three days for letters to be delivered.

A-Boscht: High Priority delivery. Within Switzerland it usually takes one day for letters to be delivered.

Express: Fast Delivery.

Iigschriibe: Certified or registered delivery. It requires a signature from the recipient.

For more information:
www.swisspost.ch

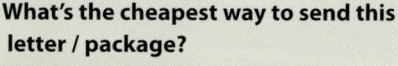

Communication

Sali zämme - your Baseldütsch survival guide

Media (News)

In the news	
Advertising	Wäärbig (f)
Article	Ardiggel (m)
Art	Kunscht (f)
Bulletin board	Aaschlagbrätt / schwarzes Brätt (n)
Cable TV	Kaabelfäärnsee (n)
Celebrity	Promi (m)
	Vip (m) *(VIP)*
Channel	Kanaal (m)
Culture	Kultuur (f)
Editor	Redaggter (m) / Herusgääber (m)
famous	beriemt / bekannt
Fashion	Moode (f)
Gossip	Grätsch (n) / Klatsch (m)
	Tratsch (m)

Survival Kit

In the news

to gossip	rätsche / klatsche / traatsche
Headlines	Schlaagziile (pl)
International news	Ussland-Noochrichte (pl)
Local news	lokaali Nöiigkäite (pl) / Lokaal-Noochrichte (pl)
Magazine	Heftli (n)
Music	Muusig (f)
National news	Inland-Noochrichte (pl)
News	Noochrichte (pl)
Newspaper	Zitig / Daageszitig (f)
Obituary	Doodesaazäig (f)
Opinion	Mäinig (f)
Photo	Fotti (f) / Fotteli (n)
Radio	Raadio (m)
Satellite	Satellit (m)
Section	Abschnitt (m) / Däil (m)
Society	Gsellschaft (f)
Sports	Spoort (m)
Talk show	Gsprööchsrundi (f) / Talk Show (engl.)
Television	Fäärnsee (n)
Television licence	Fäärnseebewilligung (f)

Communication

Sali zämme - your Baseldütsch survival guide

Food and drinks

Key survival phrases

I'm hungry.	Ich haa Hunger.
I'm thirsty.	Ich haa Durscht.
A table for two, please.	E Disch für zwäi, bitte.
Can I see the menu, please?	Hänn Sii mir d Spiiskarte, bitte?
	Kann ich emoll in d Spiiskarte luege, bitte?
I would like…	Ich möcht… / Ich hätt gärn…
with / without spicy sauce	mit schaarfer Soosse / ooni schaarfi Soosse
with / without lemon	mit / ooni Zitroone
A little…	E bitz … / E bitzeli …
A bottle of mineral water, please.	E Fläsche Wasser, bitte.
with / without ice.	Mit / ooni Iis.
A beer, please / a wheat beer, please.	E Stange, bitte. / E Wäizebier, bitte.
Can I have the bill, please?	Kaan ich zaale, bitte?
Can you split the bill?	Könne mer drennt zaale?
Did you enjoy the meal?	Ischs guet gsii? / Ischs rächt gsii? / Hets gschmeggt?
The food was good / bad.	S Ässe isch guet / nit so guet gsii.
to take away	zum Mitnää

Survival Kit

Meat

Bacon	Spägg (m)	**Pork**	Schwiinigs (n)
Beef	Rindfläisch (n)		Saufläisch (n)
Chicken	Huen (n)	**Salami**	Salaami (m)
	Güggeli (n)	**Sausage**	Wurscht (f)
Ham	Schingge (m)	**Steak**	Schteegg (n) / Blätzli (n)
Lamb	Lamm (n)		Schnitzel (n)
Liver	Lääbere (f)	**Turkey**	Druthaan (m)
Meat	Fläisch (n)	**Veal**	Kalbfläisch (n)

Food & Drinks

Meals

Appetizer	Aperitif (m)
Breakfast	Zmoorge (m)
Dessert	Desseer (m)
Dinner / Supper	Znacht (m)
Lunch	Zmittag (m)
Main course	Hauptspiis (f)
Meals	Moolzite (pl)
Snack (morning)	Znüüni (m)
Snack (afternoon)	Zvieri (m)
Starter	Voorspiis (f)

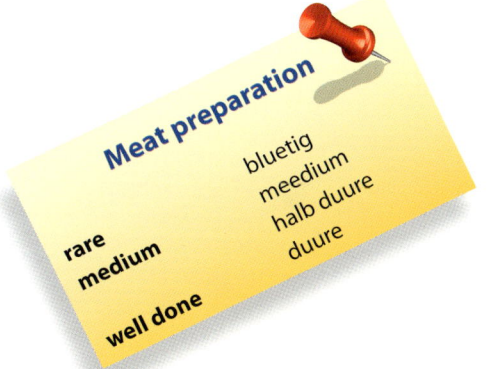

Meat preparation

rare — bluetig
medium — meedium
halb duure
well done — duure

Sali zämme - your Baseldütsch survival guide

Food & Drinks

Coffee & hot drinks

Cappuccino	Gabbudschiino / Gabbuudscho (m) *(ital.: Cappuccino)*
Coffee (with cream)	Kaffi Greem (m) *(franz.: Café crème)*
Coffee with milk	Milchkaffi (m) Schaale (f)
Espresso	Espresso (m)
Hot chocolate	Häissi Schoggi (f)
Hot milk	Häissi Milch (f)
Latte Macchiato	Latte Maggiaaddo (n) *(ital.: latte macchiato)*
Punch	Punnsch (m)
Tea	Tee (m)

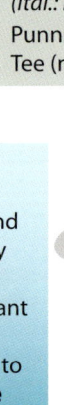

BE AWARE...
The Swiss tend to call 'Tee' any type of water infusion, so if you want a cup of black tea with milk it is better to specify: **Schwarztee mit Greem** or just **Tee Greem.**

Cold drinks

Cold drinks	Kalti Gedrängg (pl)
Apple juice	Öpfelsaft (m) Siessmoscht (m)
Coke	Goggi (n)/ Koola (n)
Grapefruit juice	Greipfruutsaft (m)
Grape juice	Druubesaft (m)
Iced tea	Iis-Tee (m)
Juice	Saft (m)
Mineral water	Mineralwasser / Blööterliwasser (n)
Orange juice	Orangschesaft (m)
Water with / without gas	Wasser mit / ooni Koolesüüri Wasser mit / ooni Blööterli
Soft drinks	alkohoolfreii Gedrängg
Cold chocolate	Kalti Schoggi (f)

Survival Kit

 Typical drinks

For children **e Siirup** (syrup with water) or **e häissi Oovi / Oovo** (hot ovaltine).

In summer typical drinks are e **Rivella** (limonade of milk serum), **e Schoorli** (apple juice with water), **e gsprützte Wisse** (white wine with water and lemon), **e Stange** (draft beer), **e Panaschee** or **e gsprützti Stange** (beer with lemonade), **e suure Moscht** (Cider).

Typical winter drinks include **e häissi Schoggi** (hot chocolate), **e Kaffi feertig** (coffee with spirit), **e Punnsch** (punch), **e Glüewii** (hot wine), **e Hypokras** (a Basel speciality of spiced wine).

In autumn you may find **Suuser** (half fermented wine).

Food & Drinks

Alcohol

Beer	Bier (n)
Champagne (a glass)	Güppli (n)
Cider	suure Moscht (m)
Digestive	Vertäilerli (m)
	Didschestiif (m)
	(franz.: digestive)
Draft beer	Stange (f)
Hot wine	Glüewii (m)
Red wine	Rootwii (m)
	Roote (m)
Spirit	Schnaps (m)
White wine	Wisswii (m)
	Wisse (m)
Wine	Wii (m)

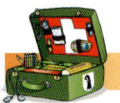

Sali zämme - your Baseldütsch survival guide

Food & Drinks

Seafood

Fish	Fisch (m)
Jack salmon	Zander (m)
Lobster	Hummer (m)
Perch	Eegli (m)
Pike	Hächt (m)
Prawns	Riisegrövette (f)
Salmon	Lachs (m)
Seafood	Meeresfrücht (pl)
Shrimp	Grövette (f)
Trout	Forälle (f)
Tuna	Doon (m)
White fish	Felche (f)

Preparations

boiled	kocht
deep fried	frittieert
fried	brääglet
grilled	grilieert
marinated	marinieert
raw	roo
roasted	grööschtet

Dairy products

Cheese	Kääs (m)
Cream	Raam (m)
Curd cheese	Quaark (m)
Milk	Milch (f)
Yoghurt	Jooguurt (n)

Bread

Baguette	Pariiserbroot (n)
Bread	Broot (n)
brown bread	dunggels Broot (n)
Cake	Kueche (m) / Doorte (f)
Croissant	Gipfeli (n)
Jam doughnut	Berliiner (m)
Pastry	Gebäck (n) / Stüggli (pl)
Pie	Wääie (f)
Roll	Schwööbli (n) /Schlumbi (n) Bröötli (n) / Büürli (n)
Sandwich	Säändwidsch (n)
Toast	Tooscht (m)
White bread	Wiissbroot (n)
Whole grain bread	Vollkoornbroot (n)

Survival Kit

 Typical Swiss and Basel dishes

Birchermiesli	Muesli with fruit, oats and yoghurt
Buttemoscht	jam from rose hip
Faschtewääie	a specially shaped roll with caraway seeds, available during Fasnacht season
Foondü *(franz.: fondue)*	Melted Cheese dipped with Bread
Lääberli und Rööschti	chopped liver and Potato tortilla
Läggerli	traditional Basel hard spice biscuit
Määlsuppe und Ziibelewääie	roasted flour soup with onion tart
Mässmogge	colourful hard candy, available during Herbschtmäss
Ragglett *(franz.: raclette)*	Melted Cheese, eaten with potatoes
Sunnereedli	a small apéro pastry, looks like a small Faschtewääie, available all year

Food & Drinks

Other food

Butter	Angge (m)	**Jam**	Gomfi (f)
Candy	Dääfeli / Dääfi (n)	**Margarine**	Maargeriine (f)
Condiment	Gwüürz (pl)	**Marmalade**	Orangschegomfi (f)
Corn	Mäis (m)	**Olive oil**	Oliivenööl (n)
Corn on the cob	Mäiskolbe (m)	**Pasta**	Däigwaare (pl)
Dressing	Salaatsoosse (f)	**Peanut butter**	Äärdnussangge (m)
Egg	Äi (n)	**Rice**	Riis (m)
Flour	Määl (n)	**Sugar**	Zugger (m)
Honey	Hoonig (m)	**Vinegar**	Essig (m)
Ice cream	Glasse (n) *(franz.: glace)*		

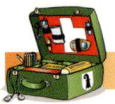

Sali zämme - your Baseldütsch survival guide

Flavours

bitter	bitter
Flavour	Gschmagg (m)
mild	mild
over salted	versalze
salty	salzig
sour	suur
spicy	schaarf
sweet	siess
tasteless	faad
	gschmaggloos

Vegetables & legumes

Beans	Boone (f)
Broccoli	Broggoli (m)
Carrots	Riebli (n)
Cauliflower	Bluemekool (m)
Eggplant	Oberschiine (f)
Garlic	Knooblauch (m)
Lentils	Linse (pl)
Legumes	Hülsefrücht (pl)
Lettuce	Kopfsalaat (m)
Onion	Ziibele (f)
Pepper	Peperooni (f)
Potatoes	Häärdöpfel (m)
Salad	Salaat (m)
Spinach	Spinaat (m)
Tomato	Domaate (f)
Vegetables	Gmies (n)

Fruits

Apple	Öpfel (m)
Banana	Banaane (f)
Cherry	Kiirsi (n)
Fruit	Frucht (f)
Lemon	Zitroone (f)
Lime	Limoone (f)
Tangerine	Manderiinli (n)
Orange	Orangsche (f)
Pear	Biire (f)
Raspberry	Himbeeri (n)
Strawberry	Äärbeeri (n)
Watermelon	Wassermeloone (f)

Shopping

Bakery	Begg (m)
	Beggerei (f)
Butcher's shop	Metzgerei (f)
Deli (catessen)	Delikatesselaade (m)
fresh	früsch
frozen	diefgfroore
Fruits of the season	früschi Frücht
Groceries	Lääbesmittel (pl)
Shop	Laade (m)
shopping	iikaufe
Supermarket	Supermäärt (m) / Iikaufszentrum (n)

Food & Drinks

Survival Kit

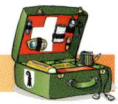

> **TIP...** It is common for a waiter to ask, after a meal, whether the food was good: **Isch es guet gsii?**
>
> This is not merely a polite question, but an opportunity to bring in some feedback.

> **TIP...** It is also common practice to share the bill if you are in a restaurant or bar with someone else. On such occasions, the waiter will usually ask you:
>
> **Zaale Sii drennt oder zämme?**
> (Are you paying separately or together?)
>
> The answer then is:
> **Drennt bitte** (separate) or
> **Alles zämme** (together).

Food & Drinks

Places to eat

Bar	Baar (f)
Coffee bar/cafe	Kaffi (n)
Canteen	Kantiine (f)
	Mensa (f)
Dining car	Spiiswaage (m)
Restaurant	Wiirtschaft (n)
	Bäiz (f)
Take away	Imbiss-Stand (m)

Diets

Diet	Diäät (f)
diabetic	diabeetisch
kosher	kooscher
halal	halal
vegan	vegaan
vegetarian	vegedaarisch

Does the meal contain pork / meat?
Hett s Schwiinigs / Fläisch drin?
Do you have vegetarian dishes?
Hänn Sii au e vegedaarischs Mönü?

ZAALE SII DRENNT ODER ZÄMME?

Sali zämme - your Baseldütsch survival guide

Health

	Key survival phrases
I don't feel well.	Miir isch nit guet / I füül mi nit wool.
I feel sick.	Miir isch schlächt.
	I füül mi grangg
Where can I find a pharmacy?	Wo hett s en Apideeg / Apodeeg?
I need something for…	I bruuch öppis geege …
Do I need a prescription?	Bruuch i e Rezäpt derfüür?
I am allergic to…	I bi allergisch uf …
Do you have something for…?	Hänn Sii öppis geege …? (fr)
I need my glasses.	I bruuch mi Brülle.
I think I'm going to be sick.	I glaub miir wirds schlächt.
I have diarrhoea.	I haa Durchfall.
I need a pill.	I bruuch e Dablette.
I'm bleeding.	S bluetet.
That doesn't look very safe.	Das seet nit grad sicher uss.
I have a headache / toothache.	Ich haa Kopfwee / Zaanwee.

Survival Kit

Key survival phrases

He / she has a concussion.	Er / Sii hett e Hiirnerschütterig.
to fall down	umfliege / umfalle / umgheie
I fell down.	Ich bi umgflooge / umgfalle / umgheit
I stumbled.	Ich bi gstolperet.
I broke my arm / leg / foot.	Ich ha miir dr Aarm / s Bäi / der Fuess broche.
My stomach / head / tooth hurts.	Mi Maage / Kopf / Zaan macht wee.
Are you pregnant?	Sinn Sii schwanger? (fr)
When was your last period?	Wenn hänn Sii s letscht Mool d Perioode ghaa?
Do you take any hormones?	Nämme Sii Hormoon? (fr)
Do you take any medicine?	Nämme Sii Medikamänt? (fr)
Do you take drugs?	Nämme Sii Drooge? (fr)
Do you drink alcohol?	Dringge Sii Alkohool? (fr)
Do you smoke?	Rauche Sii? (fr)
Do you have a private insurance?	Sinn Sii privaat versicheret? (fr)
What health insurance do you have?	Was für e Granggekasse hänn Sii? (fr)
Do you have any hereditary illnesses in your family?	Hänn Sii Erbgranggede in der Familie? (fr)

Health & Safety

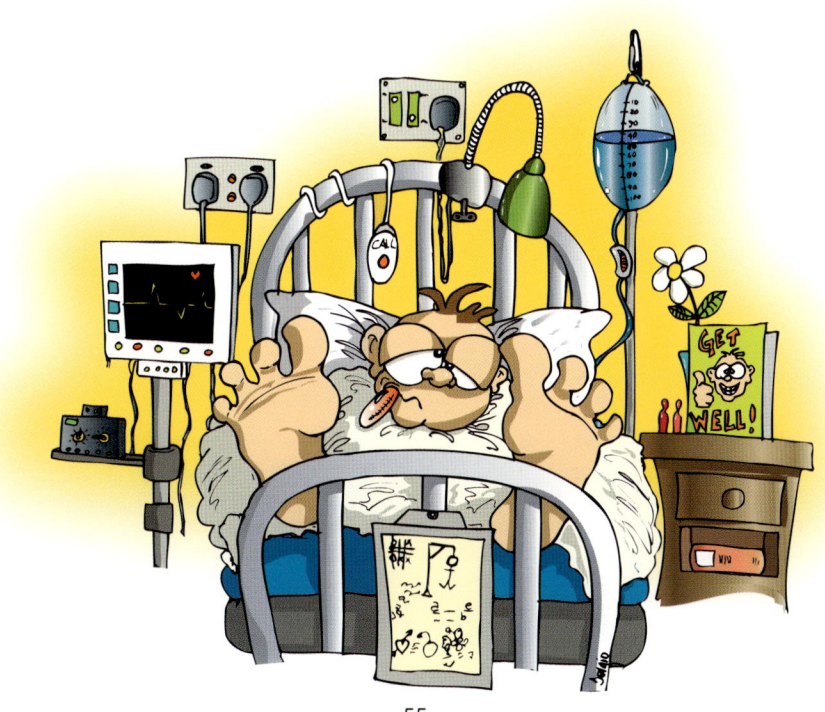

Sali zämme - your Baseldütsch survival guide

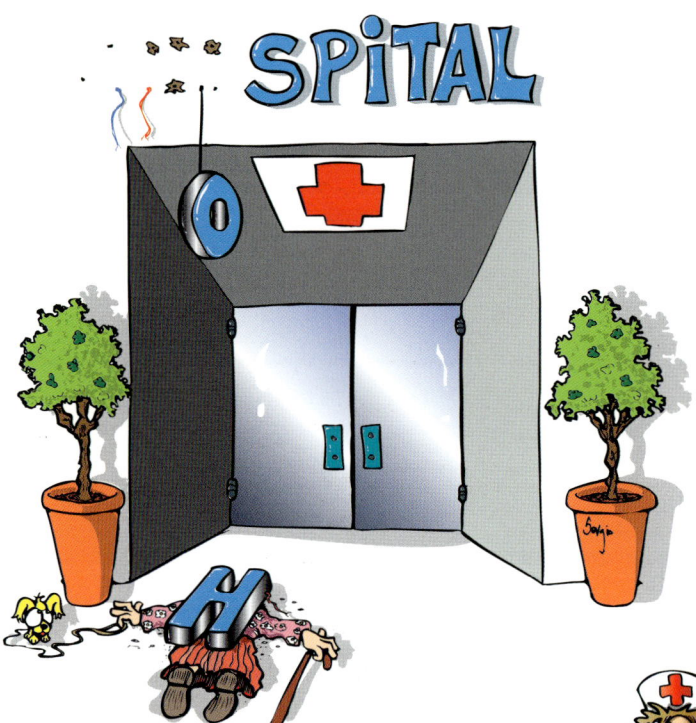

Hospital

Ambulance	Ambulanz (f)
	Granggenauti (m) / Saniteet (f)
Clinic	Kliinik (f)
Doctor	Aarzt (m), Äärztin (f) /
	Doggder (m), Doggdere (f)
Doctor's surgery	Praxis (f)
Emergency	Nootfall (m)
Emergency room	Nootuffnaam (f)
First Aid	Erschti Hiilf (f)
Hospital	Spidaal (n)
Intensive care	Intensiivstazioon (f)
Nurse *	Granggeschwechter (f) /
	Granggepflääger (m)
Patient	Baziänt (m)
	Baziäntin (f)
Prescription	Rezäpt (n)
Ward	Stazioon (f)
	Abtäilig (f)

BE AWARE... *The name for nurse has recently changed from **Granggeschweschter** (Illness sister) to **Pfläägfachfrau / maa** (Care specialist). The reason is that the profession has evolved and nurses in Switzerland didn't want to continue being associated with the nun community who were, originally, the ones doing this task.

Survival Kit

Health problems

Abscess	Abszäss (m)
allergic to ...	alergisch uff ...
Allergy	Aleergii (f)
Appendicitis	Blinddarmenzündig (f)
Asthma	Aschtma (n)
Blood pressure	Bluetdrugg (m)
Blood sugar	Bluetzugger (m)
Broken bone	Gnochebruch (m)
burn / burned	brenne / brennt / verbrennt
Cold	Verkeltig (f)
Concussion	Hiirnerschütterig (f)
contagious	aasteggend
Cramp	Grampf (m)
Diabetes	Diabeetes (f) / Zugger (m)
Diarrhoea	Durchfall (m)
Fever	Fieber (n)
Flu	Grippe (f)
Hay fever	Höischnuppe (m)
Headache	Kopfwee (n)
Infection	Enzündig (f)
Injury	Verletzig (f)
Insomnia	Schloofloosikäit (f)
Pain	Schmäärze (pl) / Wee
Parasite	Parasit (m)
Poison	Gift (n)
poisoned	vergiftet
Rabies	Dollwuet (f)
sick	grangg
Stomach ache	Buuchwee (n)
Temperature	Temperatuur (f)
to cough	hueschte
Virus	Wiirus (m)

Health remedies

Aspirin	Aschpiriin (n)
Antidote	Geegemittel (n)
Band-aid	Pfläschterli (n)
Bandage	Verband (m)
Condom	Kondoom (n) / Pariiser (m) / Gummi (m)
Contraceptive	Verhietigsmittel (n)
Cream	Greeme (f)
Drops	Dröpfli (pl)
Injection	Sprützi (f)
Massage	Massaasch (f) (franz.: massage)
Medicine	Häilmittel (n)
Operation	Operazioon (f)
Pain Killer	Schmäärzmittel (n)
Pill	Pille (f)
Sleeping pill	Schloofdablette (f)
Suppositories	Zäpfli (n)
Syrup	Siirup (m)
Tampon	Tampon (m)

Health & Safety

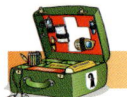

Sali zämme - your Baseldütsch survival guide

Human body

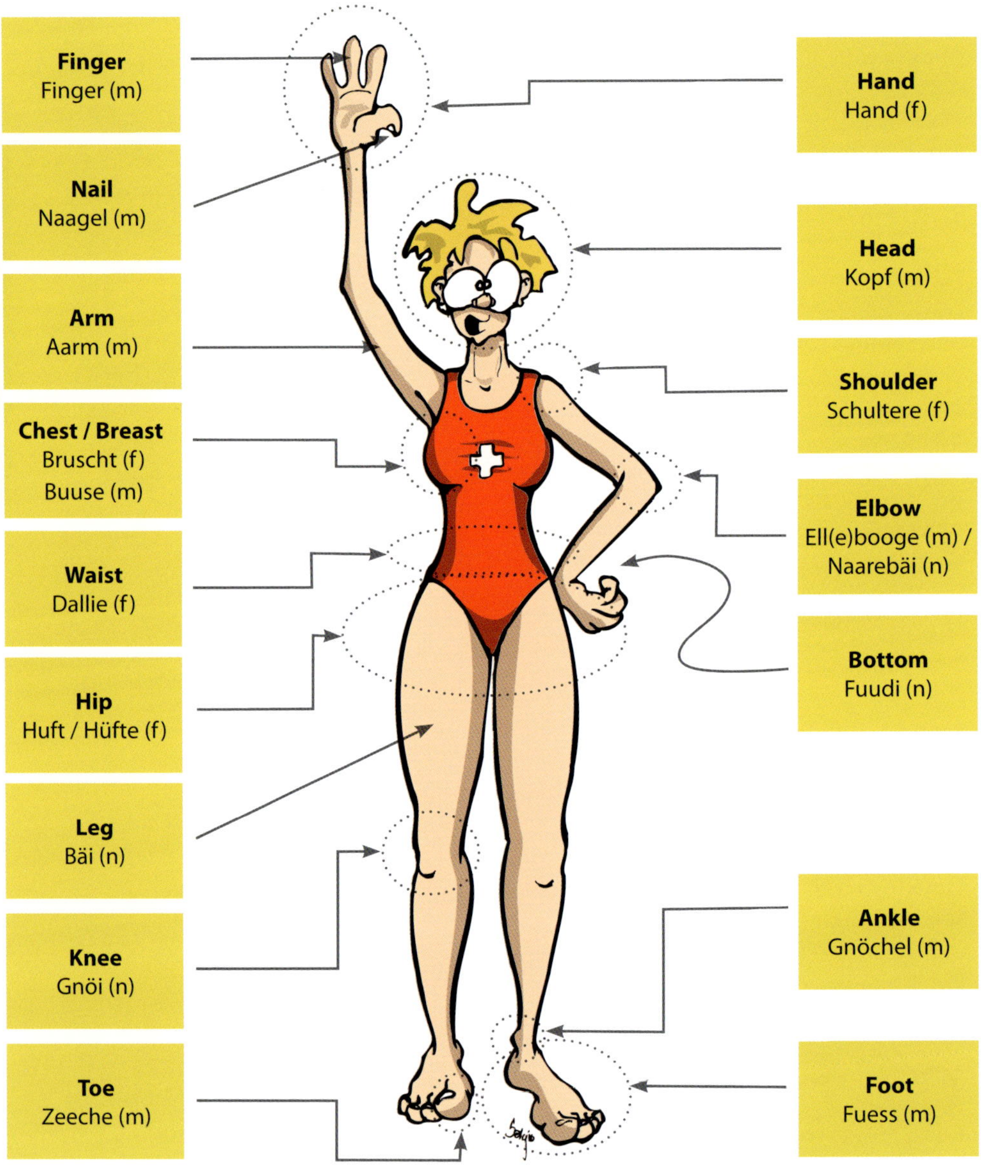

Health & Safety

English	Baseldütsch
Finger	Finger (m)
Nail	Naagel (m)
Arm	Aarm (m)
Chest / Breast	Bruscht (f) / Buuse (m)
Waist	Dallie (f)
Hip	Huft / Hüfte (f)
Leg	Bäi (n)
Knee	Gnöi (n)
Toe	Zeeche (m)
Hand	Hand (f)
Head	Kopf (m)
Shoulder	Schultere (f)
Elbow	Ell(e)booge (m) / Naarebäi (n)
Bottom	Fuudi (n)
Ankle	Gnöchel (m)
Foot	Fuess (m)

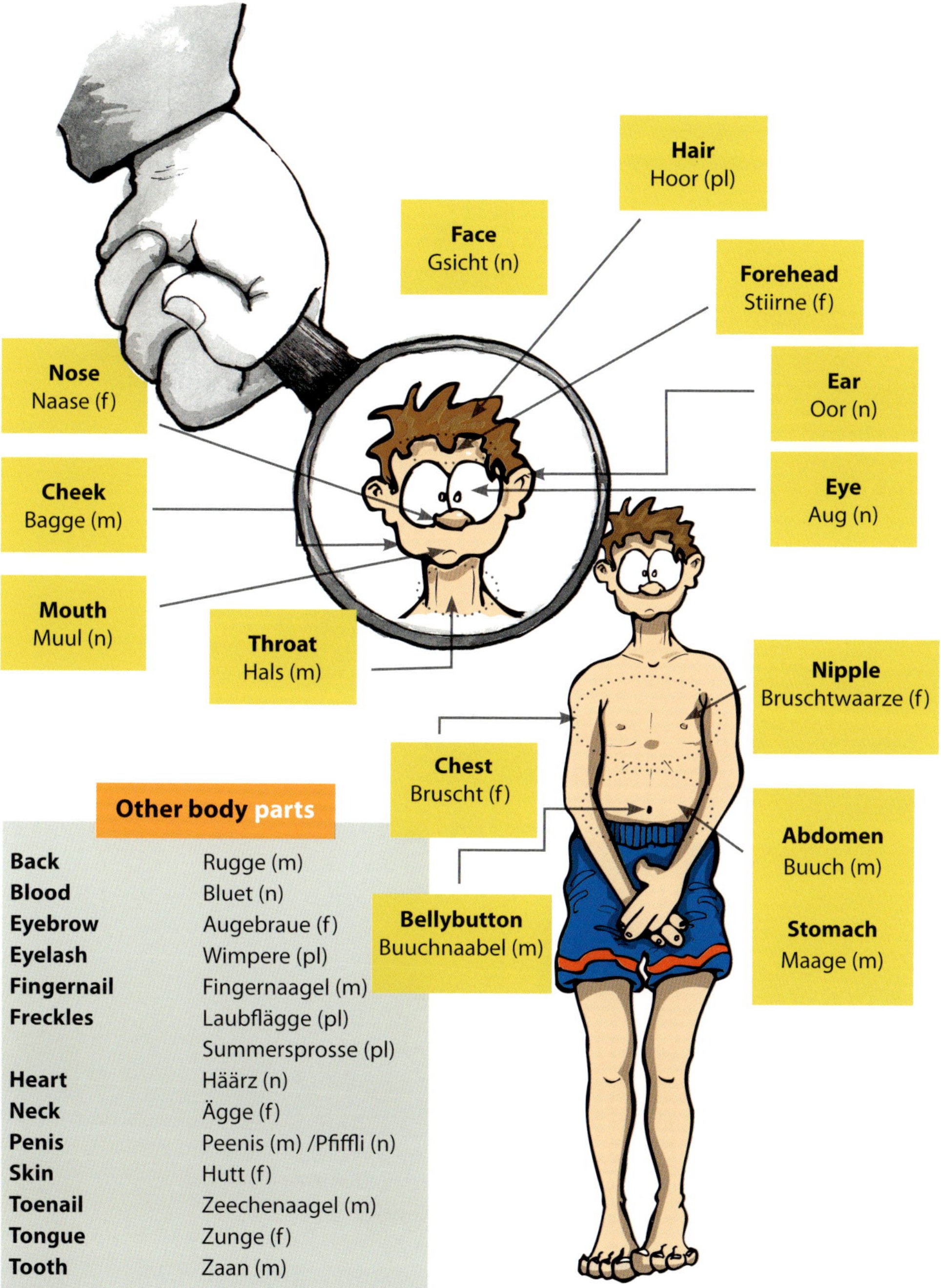

Survival Kit

Health & Safety

Hair — Hoor (pl)
Face — Gsicht (n)
Forehead — Stiirne (f)
Nose — Naase (f)
Ear — Oor (n)
Cheek — Bagge (m)
Eye — Aug (n)
Mouth — Muul (n)
Throat — Hals (m)
Nipple — Bruschtwaarze (f)
Chest — Bruscht (f)
Abdomen — Buuch (m)
Bellybutton — Buuchnaabel (m)
Stomach — Maage (m)

Other body parts

Back	Rugge (m)
Blood	Bluet (n)
Eyebrow	Augebraue (f)
Eyelash	Wimpere (pl)
Fingernail	Fingernaagel (m)
Freckles	Laubflägge (pl)
	Summersprosse (pl)
Heart	Häärz (n)
Neck	Ägge (f)
Penis	Peenis (m) /Pfiffli (n)
Skin	Hutt (f)
Toenail	Zeechenaagel (m)
Tongue	Zunge (f)
Tooth	Zaan (m)
Vagina	Vagiina (f)

Sali zämme - your Baseldütsch survival guide

> **BE AWARE...** In High German smell is **riechen** and taste is **schmecken**. Swiss Dialects, on the other hand, don't distinguish between the two, and use the verb **schmegge** for both.

Body activities

Eyes:
blink	blinzle
cry	briele / griine / hüüle
I am short-sighted.	Ich bi kurzsichtig.
I am long-sighted.	Ich bi wittsichtig.
look / watch	luege
see	see
stare	staarre / glotze
wink	zwinggere

Ears:
hear	hööre
listen	loose
wiggle	gwaggle (mit den Oore gwaggle)

Mouth:
burp	goorbse; *(for babys: göörbsle)*
cough	hueschte
kiss	schmuuse
laugh	lache
lick	lutsche
smile	lächle
speak	reede
suck	suuge
whisper	flüschtere
yawn	gääne

Hands:
fold	falte
grab	griiffe / länge / feschtheebe
press	drugge
hold	heebe
hug	umaarme
pray	bätte
shake	schüttle
touch	beriere
	aalänge

Nose:
blow one's nose	sich d Naase butze
cover	zueheebe
smell	schmegge

Skin:
blush	root wärde
dry out	uusdroggne
get wrinkles	Falte griege / bikoo
Goose bumps	Hienerhutt (f)
to get goose bumps	Hienerhutt griege / bikoo
to break out in a rash	en Ussschlaag griege / bikoo

Health & Safety

Survival Kit

Emotions

sick
grangg

bored
glangwiilt

surprised
überrascht

cold
kalt

happy
glügglig

amazed
erstuunt

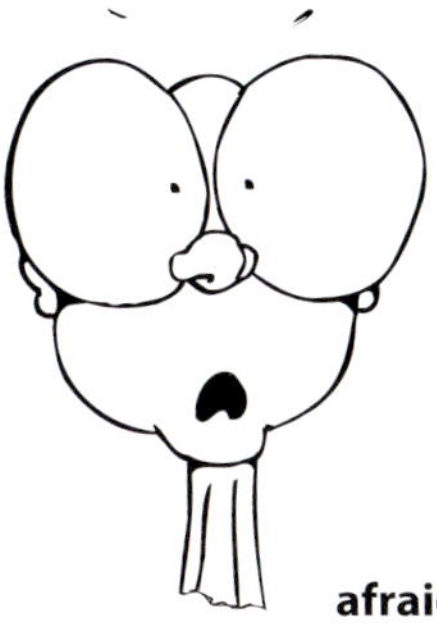

afraid
ängschtlig

jealous
iifersüchtig

sad
druurig

cool
kuul

excited
uffgreggt

cheerful
fröölig / uffgstellt / häiter

stressed
gstresst

angry
böös

Health & Safety

Sali zämme - your Baseldütsch survival guide

painful
schmäärzhaft

joyful
froo / zfriide

funny
luschtig / witzig

cosy
gmietlig

sleepy
mied / schlapp / schlööfrig

stupid
blööd / doof

lovely
häärzig

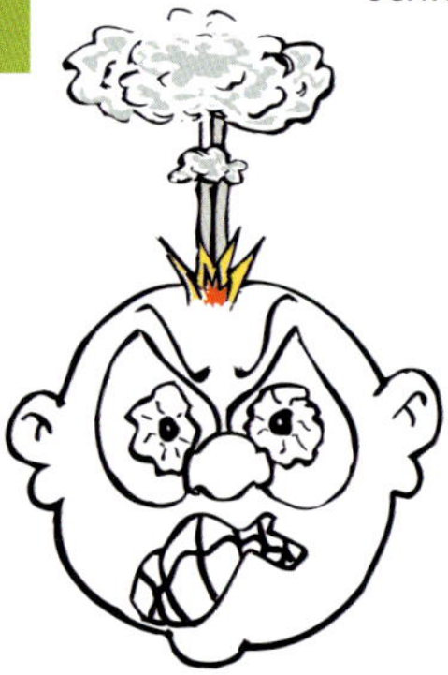

worried
besoorgt

furious
hässig

crazy
verruggt / irr / gspunne

depressed
depressiiv

Other emotions

anxious	ängschtlig
bad	schlächt
desperate	verzwiiflet
disappointed	enttüscht
embarrassed	(s isch mir) piinlig
envious	niidisch / iifersüchtig
good	guet
grateful	danggbaar
lonely	äinsaam
sentimental	sentimentaal
sexy	sexi
shy	schüüch
so-so	so soo la laa / s goot eso
vigorous	eneergisch
horny	spitz
	giggerig

Health & Safety

Survival Kit

 Swiss expressions

Deciphering Swiss expressions may be a challenge; therefore, the following illustrations can be used as a guideline:

HAPPY

SAD

ANGRY

COOL

CRAZY

Health & Safety

Sali zämme - your Baseldütsch survival guide

Emergency

Emergency

An avalanche!	E Lawiine!
Be careful!	Achtung!
Call an ambulance!	Riefe Sii d Saniteet! (fr)
	Rief d Saniteet! (inf)
Call the police!	Lütte Sii der Bolizei aa! (fr)
	Lütt der Bolizei aa! (inf)
Can someone call a doctor?	Kaa öpper ammen (en) Aarzt aalütte?
Fire!	Füür!
Help!	Hiilfe (f)!
Hurry!	Schnäll!
I am a diabetic.	Ich bi Diabeetiker / Diabeetikere.
She is pregnant.	Si isch schwanger.
I am pregnant.	Ich bi schwanger.
Is there a doctor?	Isch en Aarzt doo?
It's an emergency!	S isch e Nootfall!
Jump!	Gump! / Spring!
Get out of the way!	Göön Sii uff d Sitte! / Göön Sii uss em Wääg!/
	Göön Sii ewägg! (fr)
	Gang ewägg! / Gang uss em Wääg! /
	Uff d Sitte! / Gang uff d Sitte! (inf)
Run!	Renne Sii! (fr)
	Renn! (inf)
Someone is following me!	Öpper verfolgt mii!
Thief!	Dieb!
Watch out!	Passe Sii uff! (fr)
	Pass uff! (inf)
We need a doctor!	Mir bruuchen en Aarzt!
Where is the nearest pharmacy?	Wo isch die nägschti Apodeeg?

 Be Aware...

Fire Dept.	Füürweer (f)
Police	Bolizei (f)
Emergency	Nootfall (m)

Survival Kit

Police

Police	
Someone stole my wallet.	Mi Boortmenee isch gstoole worde.
I want to report a stolen…	Ich möcht mi gstooles … mälde.
You should go to the police.	Sii sotte zur Bolizei goo. (fr)
	Du sottsch zer Bolizei goo. (inf)
Can you please call the police?	Könnte Sii bitte der Bolizei aalütte? (fr)
I've been robbed!	Ich bi bestoole worde!
I saw what happened.	I haa gsee, waas passiert isch.
What's the fine for?	Für waas isch die Buess?
How much is the fine?	Wie hooch isch d Buess?
Where is the police station?	Wo isch der näggschti Bolizeiboschte?

Health & Safety

WARNING !

Some of the most common stolen items are:

Bag	Däsche (f)
Bicycle	Welo (n)
Briefcase	Mappe (f)
Laptop	Läptop / Läppi (m)
Mobile / Cell phone	Händi / Natel (n)
Purse	Handdäschli (n)
Wallet	Boortmenee (n)

(On page 73 you can find more useful words about money.)

Sali zämme - your Baseldütsch survival guide

Immigration and customs

Permit	Bewilligung (f)
	Genäämigung (f)
Visa	Wiisum (n)
Foreigner	Ussländer / Ussländere (m/f)
Customs	Zoll (m)
Frontier / Border	Gränze (f)
to declare (at customs)	verzolle
to immigrate	iiräise
to emigrate	ussräise
a valid visa	e gültigs Wiisum
renew a visa	e Wiisum verlengere
Residence permit	Uffenthaltsgenäämigung (f)
to apply for a visa	e Wiisum beaadraage
What kind of a visa do you have?	Was für e Wiisum hänn Sii? (fr)
I want to work in Switzerland.	Ich möcht in der Schwiz schaffe.
How can I apply for a visa?	Wie kaan ich e Wiisum beaadraage?
I have something to declare.	Ich ha öppis zem Verzolle.
I have nothing to declare.	Ich ha nüt zem Verzolle.
Do you have anything to declare?	Hänn Sii öppis zem Verzolle? (fr)
I want to stay in Switzerland for 3 months.	Ich möcht drei Mööned in der Schwiz bliibe.
I am married to a Swiss.	Ich bi mit eme Schwizer ghüüroote.
	Ich bi mit ere Schwizere ghüüroote.

 **TIP...**

The most common permits for foreigners in Switzerland are:

1. **C-Bewilligung, Niiderlassigsbewilligung:** unlimited residency in Switzerland.

2. **B-Bewilligung, Jooresbewilligung:** usually has to be renewed each year.

3. **L-Bewilligung:** Short-term Work or Residence Permit.

4. **Gränzgänger-Bewilligung:** border crosser permit.

5. **Turischtewiisum (Tourist Visa):** usually valid for three months.

For more information: **www.bfm.admin.ch**

Survival Kit

BE AWARE...
Certain things are better not done on Sundays, such as anything that could look like work (mowing your lawn, washing your car, hanging up your washing…)

YOU HAVE THE RIGHT TO REMAIN SILENT. WHATEVER YOU SAY COULD BE USED AT FASNACHT…

Health & Safety

Sali zämme - your Baseldütsch survival guide

Shopping in general

Key survival words

Bookshop	Buechhandlig (f)	**Emergency Exit**	Nootussgang (m)
	Biecherlaade (m)	**Entrance**	Iigang (m)
Brand	Maargge (f)	**Exit**	Ussgang (m)
Cashier	Kassierer (m)	**On sale**	Ussverkauf
	Kassierere (f)	**Open**	offe (adj.),
closed	zue (adj.)		uffmache (verb)
close (verb)	zuemache / zuedue /	**Price**	Briis (m)
	schliesse (verb)	**Security**	Sicherhäit (f)
complain	sich beklaage /	**Shopping bag**	Gugge / Däsche (f)
	reklamiere / joomere /	**Shopping centre**	Iikaufszentrum (n)
	mozze / wäffele	**Store**	Laade (m)
Department	Abdäilig (f)	**to buy**	kauffe / bsoorge /
Discount	reduziert /		boschte
	aabegesetzt	**to order**	bstelle
Electrical shop	Elektrogschäft (n)	**to sell**	verkauffe

BE AWARE... The biggest retailers in Switzerland own not only supermarkets, but also a vast variety of other types of shops. As they all have the same 'customer incentive' strategies, it is most likely that some shops will ask you before you pay if you have their shopping card which allows customers to collect bonus points for every purchase.

Survival Kit

Key survival shopping phrases

to go shopping	läädele
Do you have…?	Hänn Sii …? (fr)
I'm looking for…	Ich suech…
How much does it cost?	Was koschtets?
How much does this cost?	Was koschtet daas? Wie düür isch daas?
At what time do you open?	Wenn mache Sii uff?
At what time do you close?	Wenn mache Sii zue? / Ab wenn hänn Sii zue? / Bis wenn hänn Sii off?
Do you have something cheaper?	Hään Sii au öppis Günschtigers?
That's expensive!	Das isch düür!
Can you give me…?	Könnte Sii mir … gää? (fr)
Do you accept credit cards?	Nämme Sii Kreditkaarde? (fr)
I need a shopping bag.	Ich bruuch e Gugge / e Däsche.
I would like to try it on.	Kaan ich daas emoll (aa)bropiere?
How long is the warranty / guarantee?	Wie lang goot d Garantii?
I want my money back!	Ich will mi Gäld zrugg!
I will take this.	Ich nimm das.
I'm just browsing.	Ich due nur e bitz(li) ummeluege.
Where is the exit?	Wo isch der Nootussgang?
Do you have a larger / smaller size?	Hänn Sii das au grösser? gläiner?(fr)
Can you please give me a receipt?	Könnte Sii mir e Quiddig / e Beleeg gää? (fr)

Shopping

A 'BASELDÜTSCH' DICTIONARY…?
YES SIR, UPSTAIRS, IN THE CROSSWORDS AND PUZZLES SECTION…

Sali zämme - your Baseldütsch survival guide

Clothes

Shopping

Socks — Sogge (pl)
Stockings — Strümpf (pl)
Bra — Beehaa (BH) (m)
Panties — Underhoose (f)
Jeans — Tschiins (pl)
Shoes — Schue (pl)
Trousers — Hoose (f)
Belt — Gürtel (m) / Guurt (m)
Top — Oberdail (n)
Skirt — Rogg (m) / Schüp (m) / Junte (f)
T-Shirt — Liibli (n)
Tennis Shoes — Dennisschue (pl)
Shorts — Kurzi Hoose / Schoorts (pl)
Cap — Kappe (f) / Tschäpper (m)
Tie — Grawatte (f)
Hat — Huet (m)

Survival Kit

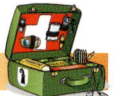

Clothes and accessories

Blouse	Bluuse (f)	Jacket	Jagge (f)
Button	Gnopf (m)	long sleeves	langeermlig
Clothing	Gläider (pl)	Scarf	Schaal (m) / Halsduech (n) / Fuulaar (n)
Coat	Mantel (m)		
Collar	Graage (m)	Shirt	Hemmli (n)
Dress (noun)	Gläid / Gläidli (n)	short sleeves	kurzeermlig
dress (verb)	aaleege	Suit	Goschdüüm (n) / Gwändli (n) / Schaale (f) / Aazuug (m)
dressed	aaglegt		
Evening dress	Oobegläid / Gläid (n)	Underwear	Underwösch (f)
Gloves	Händsche (pl)	Wallet	Boortmenee (n)

*I DON'T CARE IF WE WORK IN THE CENTRE OF BASEL... FASNACHT IS STILL **NOT** A BUSINESS DRESS CODE...*

Clothing materials

The following is a list of the most common textiles:

Cotton	Bauele / Baumwulle (f)
Leather	Lääder (n)
Linen	Liine (f)
Nylon	Näilen (n)
Polyester	Polijeschter (m)
Silk	Siide (f)
Wool	Wulle (f)

Shopping

Sali zämme - your Baseldütsch survival guide

Money and banking

Money

Money	Gäld (n)	**Interest**	Zins (m)
Bank	Bangg (f)	**invest money**	Gäld inweschtiere
Bank account	Banggkonto (n)	**Investment**	Inweschtizioon (f)
Banknotes	Banggnoote (f)	**Loan**	Darleehe (n)
Cash	Baar / Baargäld (n)	**Loss**	Verluscht (m)
Cash machine	Gäldautomat / Banggomaat / Boschtomaat (m)	**Payment**	Zaalig (f)
		Profit	Profitt (m)
		Rappen *	Rappe (m)
Cheque	Schegg (m)	**Savings account**	Spaarkonto (n)
Coin	Münze (f)	**Signature**	Underschrift (f)
Counter	Schalter (m)	**Small change**	Münz (n) / Münze (pl)
Credit card	Kreditkaarde (f)	**Swiss franc**	Schwizer Frangge (m)
Currency	Wäärig (f)	**to pay**	zaale
Debit card	Eezee-Kaarte (f) (EC-Kaarte) Boschtkaarte (f)	**to save**	spaare
		to spend	ussgää / verbutze / vergänggerle
Deposit	Deppo (n) Hinderleegig (f)	**to transfer**	überwiise
		Travelers cheques	Schegg (pl)
earn money	Gäld verdiene	**to withdraw**	abheebe
Exchange rate	Wäggselkuurs (f)		
Income	Iikomme (n)	* 100 Rappen = 1 Swiss Franc	

Shopping

Survival Kit

Money, banks and exchange office

What's the exchange rate today for British pounds / dollars?
Wie isch hütt der Kuurs für Britischi Pfund / Dollar?

Can you please change this banknote for small change?
Könnte Sii mir das Nöötli wäggsle? (fr)

Do you have change for this?
Hätte Sii mir Münz für daas? (fr)

I don't have any money.
Ich ha käi Gäld.

Your cash machine kept my card!
Der Automaat het mi Kaarte iizooge!

How many francs do I get for ... dollars ?
Wie viil Schwizer Frangge grieg ich für ... Doller?

I would like to open a bank account / savings account.
Ich möcht e Banggkonto/ Spaarkonto erröffne.

to put money aside
Gäld spaare / uff d Site leege / uff die hochi Kante leege

Shopping

Sali zämme - your Baseldütsch survival guide

Transportation

Travelling

BVB survival phrases

Where is the tram/bus timetable?	Wo isch der Drämmli-/Bus-Faarblaan?
Where is the next tram/bus stop?	Wo isch die näggschti Dramm-/Bus-Haltstell?
Would you like to sit down?	Möchte Sii sitze/absitze/aanesitze?
May I sit down?	Könnt ich bitte sitze/absitze/aanesitze?
What's the name of this stop?	Wie häisst die Haltstell?
Does this tram go to …….?	Goot/Faart das Dramm/Drämmli uf/an …?
Which tram takes me to …..?	Weeles Dramm/Drämmli goot/faart uf/an …?
Do you need help?	Kaan ich Iine hälfe? / Bruuche Sii Hilf?
Could you please hold the door open for me?	Könnte Sii mir bitte (dr Gnopf) drugge?
Could you please help me with my stroller/bags?	Könnte Sii mir bitte mit mim Koffer/Gepäck hälfe?
Can you help me get a ticket from the ticket machine please?	Könne Sii mir hälfe e Billjee uusezloo?
Excuse me, your bicycle is on top of my dog	Exgüüsi, Iir Welo ligt uf mim Hund oobe.

Survival Kit

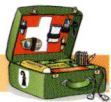

How to use the BVB tram/bus ticket machines in Basel

use this side if you pay full fare

short-distance tickets (up to 4 stops) touch here to see the valid stops

use this side if you have a Swiss half-fare travel card, for dogs, or children up to six-years-old

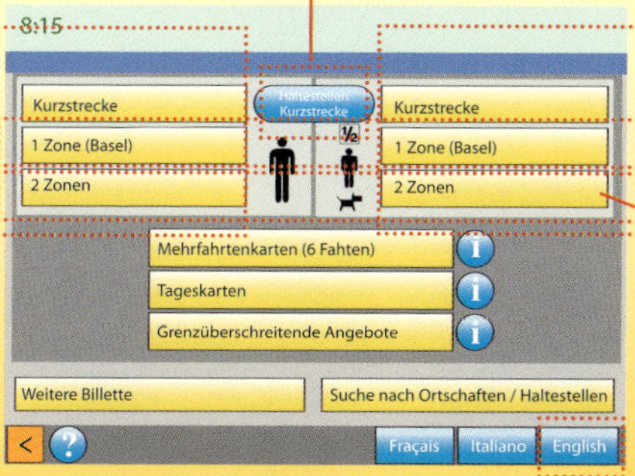

'1 zone' means more than 4 stops but within Basel's zone 10

'2 zones' means for going to the outskirts beyond zone 10

touch here for text in **English**

BE AWARE... Tickets have to be bought before departure. There is no possibility to buy tickets on trains, busses and trams.

TIP... Panorama ticket: trams 15 and 16 take you on a round-trip tour of the main sites of Basel

U-Abo: this is a travel card allowing unlimited transport for a certain month or year

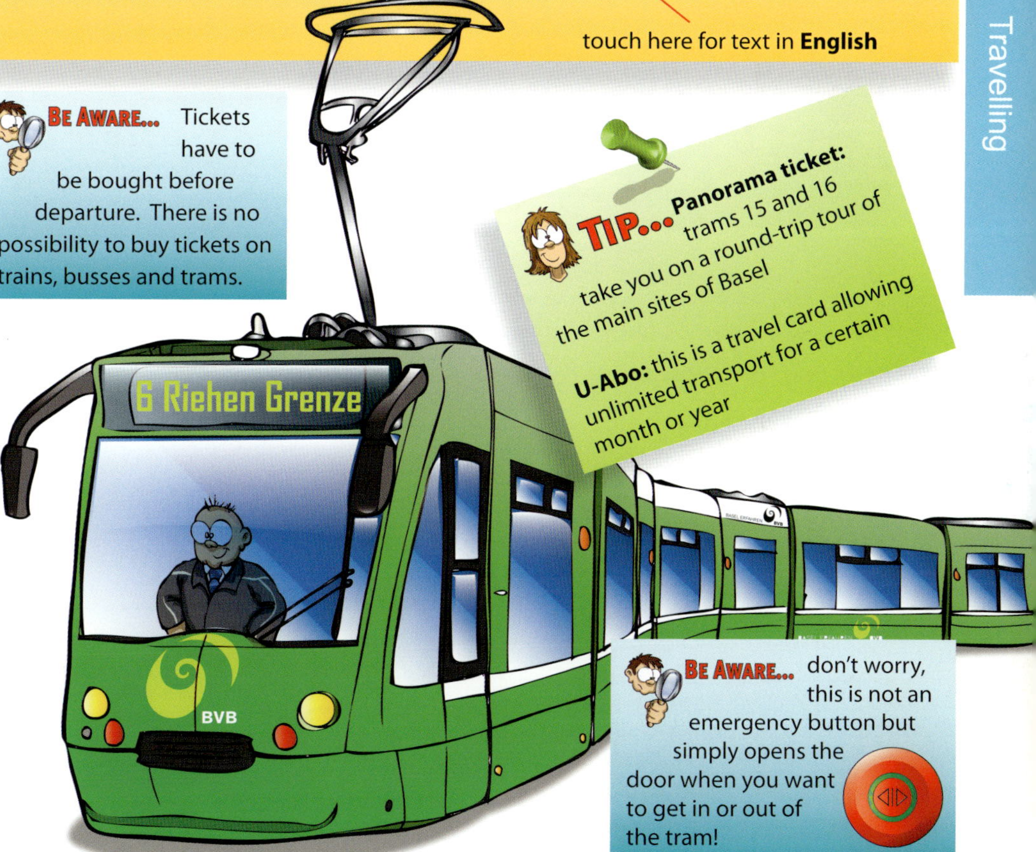

BE AWARE... don't worry, this is not an emergency button but simply opens the door when you want to get in or out of the tram!

Travelling

Sali zämme - your Baseldütsch survival guide

Key survival phrases

I have lost my ticket.	Ich haa mi Billjee verloore.
I bought the wrong ticket.	Ich haan e falschs Billjee kauft.
Does this train / bus stop at…?	Haltet dä Zuug / Bus in … / bi …?
When does the next train for…leave?	Wenn faart der näggschti Zuug uf…?
Is this the train / bus to….?	Isch daas der Zuug / Bus uf …?
At what time does the train from…arrive?	Wenn kunnt der Zuug vo … aa?
On what platform does the next train for… leave?	Uf wellem Gläis faart der Zuug uf…?

Travelling

ALLI BILLJEE BITTE

Translation: Tickets please.

TIP... There are different tickets with special price offers to travel around Switzerland. The main offers are:

GA (Generaalabonnemänt): an unlimited ticket valid for most of public transport in Switzerland.

Halbtaxabonnemänt: a card that allows you to buy tickets for most public transport at half price.

Daageskaarte: a one-day ticket valid for most of public transport in Switzerland.

Famiiliekaarte: a ticket for families which offers reduced prices for children.

For more information: **www.sbb.ch/en**

WARNING !

What ticket controllers will usually ask...

Alli Billjee bitte!
All tickets please (request to show tickets)
Wohäär kömme Sii?
Where are you coming from?
Wo sinn Sii iigstiige?
Where did you get on?
Wo aane faare Sii?
Where are you going?
Hänn Sii e gültigs Billjee?
Do you have a valid ticket?

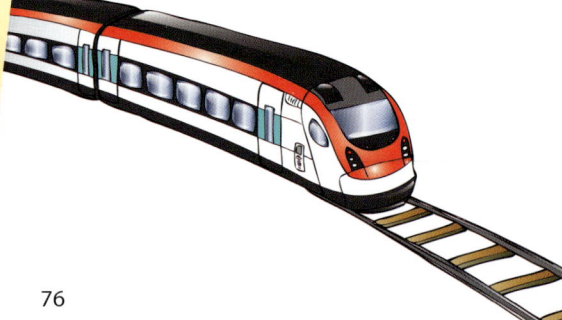

Survival Kit

Key survival phrases

A ticket to..., please.	E Billjee uf ..., bitte.
How much does a ticket to...cost?	Was koscht(et) e Billjee uf ...?
Window / aisle	Am Fänschter / bim Gang
No Smoking	Nichtraucher
One way ticket	äifach / nur aane / nur hii
Return ticket	hii und zrugg / aane und zrugg / rötuur
Do I have to change trains?	Muess i umstiige?
Where do I have to change...?	Woo muess i umstiige?
The train / bus is delayed.	Der Zuug / Bus hett Verspöötig.
on foot	z Fuess
by car / by bike	mit em Auto / Welo
by plane / by train	mit em Flugzüüg / mit em Zuug
The flight is cancelled.	Der Fluug isch annuliert.
Where can I get a taxi?	Wo hetts e Taxi?

Travel words

		Passport	Bass (m)
Aeroplane	Fluugzüüg (n)	Petrol	Benziin (n) / Moscht (m)
Arrival	Aakunft (f)	Petrol station	Tankstell (f)
Bus	Bus (m)	Platform	Perron (n)
Bus station	Busbaanhoof (m)	Rucksack	Ruggsagg (m)
Bus stop	Bushaltstell (f)	Space	Blatz (m) / Ruum (m)
Bus ticket	Busbilljee (n)	to reserve	reserviere
Car	Auto (n)	Tourist	Turischt (m)
City map	Stadtblaan (m)		Turischtin (f)
Delay	Verspöötig (f)	Train	Zuug (m)
Departure	Abräis (f)	Train ticket	Zugbilljee (n)
Driving licence	Faaruuswiis (m)	Train station	Baanhoof (m)
	Billjee (n)	Track	Gläis (n)
drive too fast	raase	Service area	Raschtblatz (m)
Highway/Motorway	Autobaan (f)		Raschtstett (f)
leave	abfaare	Speed camera	Radaar (m)
land	lande	Speed limit	Gschwindigkäits-
Luggage	Gepäck (n)		begränzig (f)
Plane ticket	Fluugbilljee (n)	to get on a bus	in Bus iistiige
Passenger	Passaschier (m) /	to get off a bus	us em Bus uusstiige
	Faargascht		

Travelling

Sali zämme - your Baseldütsch survival guide

Directions

Key survival phrases

to the left	nach linggs
to the right	nach rächts
around the corner	um en Egge
across (the bridge, the crossover)	über d Brugg, d Überfierig
(X) streets from here	(X) Strosse witter
I'm looking for…	Ich suech …
I think I am lost.	Ich glaub ich haa mi verloffe.
Where? / in which direction?	Woo? / In weeli Richtig?
Do you know where… is?	Wüsse Sii, woo … isch? (fr)
	Wäisch (du), woo … isch? (inf)
Could you tell me the way to ….?	Könnte Sii mir saage, woo … isch? (fr)
How far is it to walk / to drive?	Wie wiit isch das zem Lauffe / zem Faare?
Go straight on as far as the church.	Göön Sii graaduss bis zer Kirche. (fr)
Go along the river.	Lauffe Sii em Fluss entlang. (fr)
along the street	der Strooss entlang

Continued on the next page….

Travelling

Survival Kit

Key survival phrases

go up.	Si mien uffe.
go down.	Si mien aabe.
up the stairs	d Stäägen uffe
down the escalator	d Rolldräppen aabe
go across the street	über d Strooss
Is it far / close?	Ischs wit? Nooch?
behind the house	hinderem Huus / hinder s Huus
in front of the house	voorem Huus / voor s Huus
through the market	über der Määrtblatz
to the station / to the church	bis zum Baanhoof / zer Kirche
passing the school	am Schuelhuus verbii
leaving the village	us em Doorf uuse
entering the village	ins Doorf iine
not far at all	nit wit / nur e Katzesprung / e Stäiwurf *

* only a stone's throw

Key survival words

up	uffe
down	aabe
left	linggs
right	rächts
here	doo
there	döört
straight on	graaduss
Map	Kaarte (f)
	Stadtblaan (f)

Travelling

Some reference points

Bridge	Brugg (f)
Cathedral	Kathedraale (f) / Münschter (n)
Church	Kirche (f)
Corner	Egge (m)
Crossing	Grüzzig (f) / Abzwiigig (f)
Mosque	Moschee (f)
School	Schuelhuus (n) / Schuel (f)
Street	Strooss (f)
Synagogue	Siinagooge (f)
Traffic light	Ample (f)

Sali zämme - your Baseldütsch survival guide

Prepositions

TIP... When it comes to directions, prepositions are the most useful words to provide accurate information. This list shows the most common prepositions in Baseldütsch.

Key prepositions

English	Baseldütsch	English	Baseldütsch
across from / opposite	wisawii / geegenüüber	from	us / vo
		from / of	vo
after / according to	noch	in / into	in
against / into	geege	in front of	voor
along	entlang	on (horizontal surfaces)	uff
around	um	over / above / across	über
at / by	bim / bi	through	dur
at / on (vertical surfaces)	am / an	to	zum / zur
behind	hinder	under / beneath	under
beside / next to	nääbe	until / by	bis
between	zwüsche	with / by (transport)	mit
for	für	without	ooni

Travelling

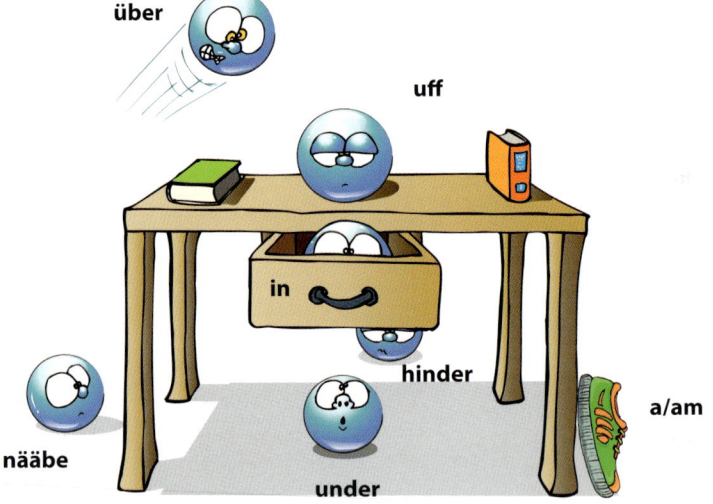

über · uff · in · hinder · nääbe · under · a/am · vor

Survival Kit

Hotel

Key survival phrases

Do you have a room?	Hänn Sii non e Zimmer frei? (fr)
Single / Double room please.	En Äinzelzimmer / e Doppelzimmer, bitte.
Is breakfast included?	Ischs Zmoorge im Briis derbii?
with a view of the Rhein	mit Sicht uf e Rhii
Can I have a morning call?	Könne Sii mii delefoonisch wegge?
I want to check out.	Ich möcht uss-tschegge / zaale.
Can I have the key to the room?	Der Schlüssel fürs Zimmer … , bitte.
How much is it a night?	Wie viil koschtes / machts pro Nacht?
I will stay for … nights.	Ich bliib für … Nächt.
I'd like to book …	Ich möcht … bueche.
I reserved a room in the name of ….	Ich haan e Zimmer für … reserviert.
At what time is breakfast served?	Wenn ischs Zmoorgenässe?
a quiet room	e rueigs Zimmer
a room with bath / with bath nearby	e Zimmer mit Baad / mit Etaascheduschi
Youth hostel	Juugendheerbärg (f)

Travelling

Sali zämme - your Baseldütsch survival guide

Hotel words

English	Baseldütsch
B&B	B&B (n)
Bed	Bett (n)
Bed cover	Bettaazug (m)
Bike parking	Welo-Paarkblatz (m)
Car parking	Auto-Paarkblatz (m)
Check in	ii-tschegge
Check out	uss-tschegge
Children friendly	kinderfründlig
Concierge	Gonsiersch *(franz.: concierge)*
Double bed	Doppelbett (n)
Full board	Vollbangsioon (f)
Gym	Fitnessruum (m)
Hair dryer	Föön (m)
Half board	Halbbangsioon (f)
Key	Schlüssel (m)
Lift	Lift (m)
Lobby	Hotelhalle (f)
Non-smoking room	Nichtraucher-Zimmer (n)
Pet friendly	dierfründlig
Pillow	Küssi (n)
Reception	Ressepsion (f) *(franz.: réception)*
Room	Zimmer (n)
Room service	Zimmermäitli (f) / Zimmer-Seerwis (m)
Slippers	Fingge (pl)
Swimming pool	Schwimmbaad (n) / Bassä (n) *(franz.: bassin)*
Towel	Diechli (n) Wäschblätz (m)
Twin beds	Zwäi Äinzelbetter (pl)
Wake up call	Wegg-Delifon (m)

Survival Kit

Outdoors

Travelling

Geography

		Hill	Hüügel (m)	**River**	Fluss (m)
City	Stadt (f)	**Island**	Insle (f)	**Sea**	Meer (n)
	Innerstadt (f)	**Lake**	See (m)	**State**	Staat (m)
Continent	Kontinänt (m)	**Mountain**	Bäärg (m)	**County**	Kantoon (m)
Country	Land (n)	**Ocean**	Ozeaan (m)	**Town**	Stadt (f)
Field	Fäld (n)	**Park**	Paark (m)	**Valley**	Daal (n)
Forest	Wald (m)	**Path**	Wääg (m)	**Village**	Dörfli (n)
Geography	Geografii (f)	**Peak**	Gipfel (m)	**World**	Wält (f)

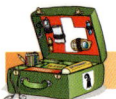

Sali zämme - your Baseldütsch survival guide

Outdoor snow terms

boarding	snööbe / boorde	**Ski instructor**	Schiileerer (m)
Chair lift	Sässelilift (m)		Schiileerere (f)
Cross country skiing	langlauffe	**Ski lift**	Schiilift (m)
easy hill to ski	Idiottehüügel (m)	**Ski poles**	Stögg (pl)
Equipment	Ussrüschtig (f)	**Ski school**	Schiischuel (f)
I like skiing.	Ich faar gärn Schii.	**Ski tour**	Schiituure mache
pretty girl skiing	Schneehääsli (n)	**skiing**	schiifaare
Ski	Schii (m)	**Snow shoeing**	Schneeschue lauffe
Ski boot	Schiischue (m)		

Travelling

Survival Kit

Other snow terms and phrases

Partying and drinking after skiing	Apre-Schii (n)
Are you a good snowboarder?	Kasch (du) guet snööbe / boorde? (inf)
I am a snowboarder.	Ich bin e Snööber.
off the marked slope	nääbe der Pischde

Outdoor mountain terms

Bicycle	Welo (n)
Camping	Kämping (n)
Direction sign	Wägwiiser (m)
driving	Auto faare
Altimeter	Hööemässer (m)
Grill area	Füürstell (f)
hiking	wandere
Hiking path	Wanderwääg (m)
Hiking shoes	Wanderschue (pl)
paragliding	Gläitschirm fliege
Picnic	Piggnigg (n)
Provisions	Proviant (m)
Swiss army knife	Saggmässer (n)
walking	lauffe

Travelling

TIP...
1. Hiking trails (**Wanderwääg**) in Switzerland are always marked with a yellow rhombus.
2. If you are a keen hiker or an outdoor person, be sure to become a member of Rega (Swiss air rescue).

website: **www.rega.ch**

Other mountain terms and phrases

Is it steep?	Ischs stäil?
How long do we have to climb?	Wie lang isch der Uffstiig?
How far away is the restaurant?	Wie wiit ischs no bis ze der Bäiz?

Sali zämme - your Baseldütsch survival guide

Entertainment

Key survival phrases

What are your hobbies?	Was hänn Sii für Hobbis? (fr)
	Was hesch (du) für Hobbis? (inf)
What do you do in your spare time?	Was mache Sii in lirer Freiziit? (fr)
	Was machsch (du) in diner Freiziit? (inf)
What do you like to do the most?	Was mache Sii am liebschte? (fr)
	Was machsch (du) am liebschte? (inf)
I like cooking / eating / travelling.	Ich due gärn koche / ässe / räise.
What's your favourite food?	Was isch di Lieblingsspiis? (inf)
I collect stamps.	Ich sammle Briefmaargge.
I like listening to music / watching TV.	Ich loos gärn Muusig. / Ich lueg gärn Fäärnsee.
I read novels/ cartoons / the newspaper.	Ich liis Romään / Komiggs / d Zittig.
I listen to classical music.	Ich loos gärn klassischi Muusig.
I jog regularly.	Ich gang reegelmäässig go tschogge.
I go twice a week to the gym.	Ich gang zwäimoll pro Wuchä ins Fitnessstudio.
I like playing golf / the piano / the violin.	Ich spiil gärn Golf / Klavier / Giige.

Travelling

TIP... To give preferences, you may use the adverb **'gäärn'**, which is always placed after the verb: **Ich iss gäärn Banaane** (I like eating bananas).

TIP... Frequency is expressed with **moll**: **äimoll** (once), **zwäimoll** (twice), **dreimoll, viermoll** etc. **Pro** means per, **pro Wuche** (per week), **pro Moonet** (per month) etc.

Survival Kit

Travelling

Key survival words

Beach	Strand (m)	**Museum**	Museeum (n)
Book	Buech (n)	**Music**	Muusig (f)
Cinema	Kiino (n)	**Opera**	Oopere (f)
Concert	Konzäärt (n)	**Party**	Fescht (n)
dancing	danze	**Theatre**	Theaater (n)
Discotheque	Disco (f)	**to collect (cars)**	(Auto) sammle
Entertainment	Underhaltig (f)	t**o fish**	fische
Event	Aaloss (m)	**to gamble**	spiile
Exhibition	Uss-stellig (f)	**to play**	spiile
Fitness	Fitness	**to play football**	schutte
Game	Spiil (n)	**to read**	lääse
Humour	Humoor (m)	**to swim**	schwimme
Joke	Witz (m)	**Wind surfing**	Windsöörfe
Library	Bibliotheek (f)	**Zoo**	Zolli / Zoo (m)
Magic	Zauberei (f)		
	zaubere (Verb)		

 Sali zämme - your Baseldütsch survival guide

 Swiss Traditions

blowing the alpenhorn	Alphorn bloose
Carnival	Faasnacht (f)
swinging flags	Faaneschwinge
Swiss accordion	Handöörgeli (n)
Swiss traditional music	Ländler (m)
Swiss wrestling	schwinge
throwing stones	Stai stosse
yodelling	joodle

TIP... **Lieblings** means favourite and can be combined with lots of other words: **Lieblingsässe** (favourite food), **Lieblingsfilm** (favourite movie), **Lieblingsbäiz** (favourite restaurant).

Travelling

Survival Kit

Travelling

 Basel traditions

Crossing borders	über d Gränze goo
Drumming and playing piccolo	drummle und pfiffe
Eating asparagus in the Elsass	im Elsass go Spaarsen ässe
Kissing on the Pfalz	Schmuusen uf dr Pfalz
Swimming in the Rhine	Schwimmen im Rii / Riischwimme

For these and more traditions and events, see also 'Basel all year round' on the inside back cover.

Sali zämme - your Baseldütsch survival guide

Family

Family tree

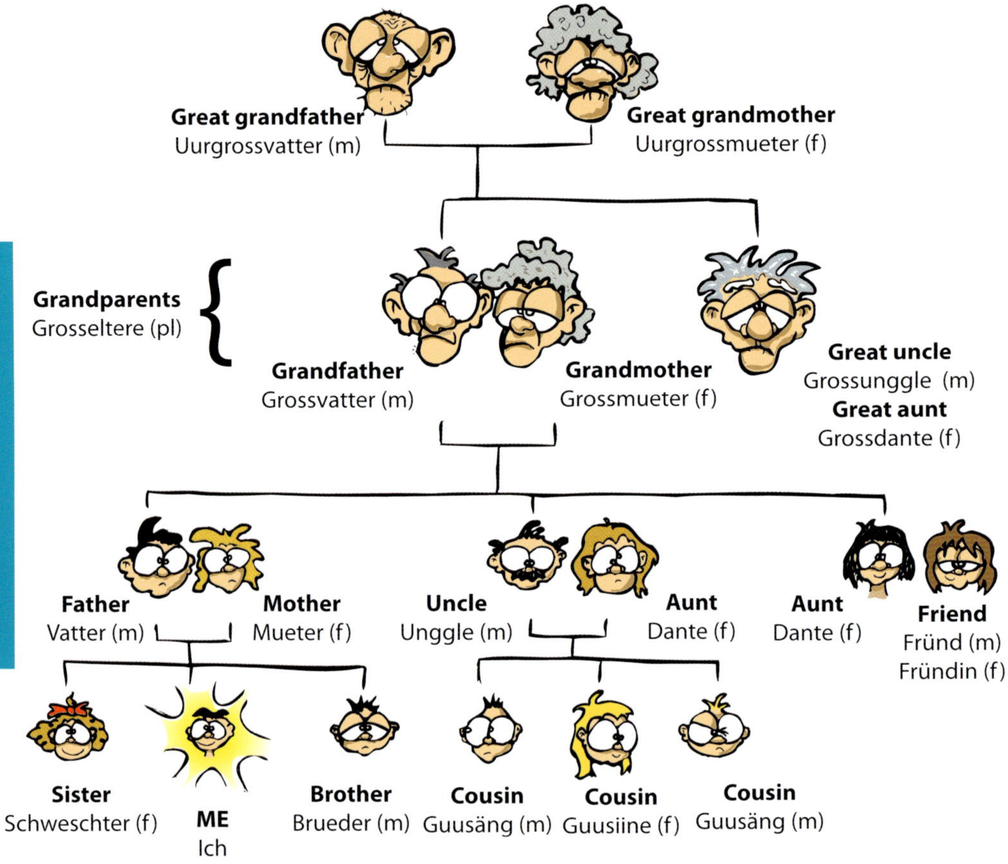

Great grandfather Uurgrossvatter (m)
Great grandmother Uurgrossmueter (f)

Grandparents Grosseltere (pl)

Grandfather Grossvatter (m)
Grandmother Grossmueter (f)

Great uncle Grossunggle (m)
Great aunt Grossdante (f)

Father Vatter (m)
Mother Mueter (f)
Uncle Unggle (m)
Aunt Dante (f)
Aunt Dante (f)
Friend Fründ (m) Fründin (f)

Sister Schweschter (f)
ME Ich
Brother Brueder (m)
Cousin Guusäng (m)
Cousin Guusiine (f)
Cousin Guusäng (m)

People

Marital status

Marital Status	Ziviilstand (m)	**separated**	drennt
single	leedig / elläisteehend	**divorced**	gschiide
		Widow	Witwe (f)
engaged	verlobt	**Widower**	Witwer (m)
married	ghüüroote	**widowed**	verwitwet

Survival Kit

Other family relations

Brother-in-law	Schwooger (m)
Father-in-law	Schwiigervatter (m)
Grandchild	Grosskind (n)
Mother-in-law	Schwiigermuetter (f)
Nephew	Neffe / Nöwöö (m)
Niece	Nichte (f)
Relatives	Verwandti (pl)
Siblings	Gschwischterti (pl)
Sister-in-law	Schwöögere (f)
Son-in-law	Schwiigersoon (m)
Twins	Zwilling (pl)

People

Useful family terms

Family get together	Familiezämmekunft (f) / Familieschluuch (m)
We are related.	Mir sind verwandt.
My family is important to me.	Mi Familie isch mir wichtig.
I am a family person.	Ich bin e Familiemensch.
My brother's / sister's name is …	Mi Brueder / Schweschter häisst …
Parent's home	Elterehuus (n)
My family lives in …	Mi Familie läbt in …
Give my regards to your family.	Griess di Familie vo mir. (inf)
How is your family?	Wie goots der Familie? (inf)
We are going to have a baby.	Mir griegen e Kind.

Sali zämme - your Baseldütsch survival guide

Babies

Key survival words

baby	Buschi / Buscheli (n)	sleeper / "onesie"	Strampelhoose (m)
baby bottle	Schobbe (m)	stuffed animal	Blüschdier (n)
baby sling	Draagduech (n)	swing	Giigampfi (f)
bedtime story	Guetnacht- Gschichtli (n)		Ritti (f)
bib	Ässmänteli (n)	to bottle feed	der Schobbe gää
changing table	Wiggeldisch (n)	to change a baby	Windle wäggsle
cot / crib	Kinderbett (n)	to count sheep	Schööfli zelle
dummy / pacifier	Nuggi (m)	to nurse	stille
kindergarten	Kindsgi / Kindergaarte / Hääfelischuel (m)	to suck one's thumb	am Duume suuge
		to teeth	zaane
mash / baby food	Breili (n)	to vaccinate	impfe
nappies / diapers	Windle (pl)	to weep / to cry	briele / griine / hüüle / schreie
pediatrician	Kinderaarzt (m) / Kinderäärztin (f)		
		Twins	Zwilling
pram / stroller	Kinderwaage (m)		

Key survival phrases

Do you have a fridge where I can store this milk?
Hänn Sii en Iiskaschte, won ich d Milch könnt driidue?
Could you please warm this bottle for me?
Könnte Sii mir dä Schobbe weerme?
Where can I change the baby?
Wo kaan ich mi Buschi wiggle?
Where can I nurse my baby in private?
Wo kaan ich mi Buschi ungstöört stille?
Do you have a high chair?
Hänn Sii e Kindersitzli?
Where is the children's department?
Wo isch d Kinderabdäilig?
Is there a play ground close by?
Hetts in der Nööchi e Spiilblatz?

Survival Kit

Age

Baby girl
Mäiteli (n)

Baby boy
Biebli (n)

Girl
Mäitli (n)

Boy
Bueb (m)

Teenager
Tiini (m)

Young woman
jungi Frau (f) /
Froläin (n)

Young man
Junge Maa (m) /
Buursch (m)

Adult
Erwaggseni (f)

Adult
Erwaggsene (m)

Old woman
alti Frau (f)

Old man
alte Maa (m)

People

93

Sali zämme - your Baseldütsch survival guide

Home

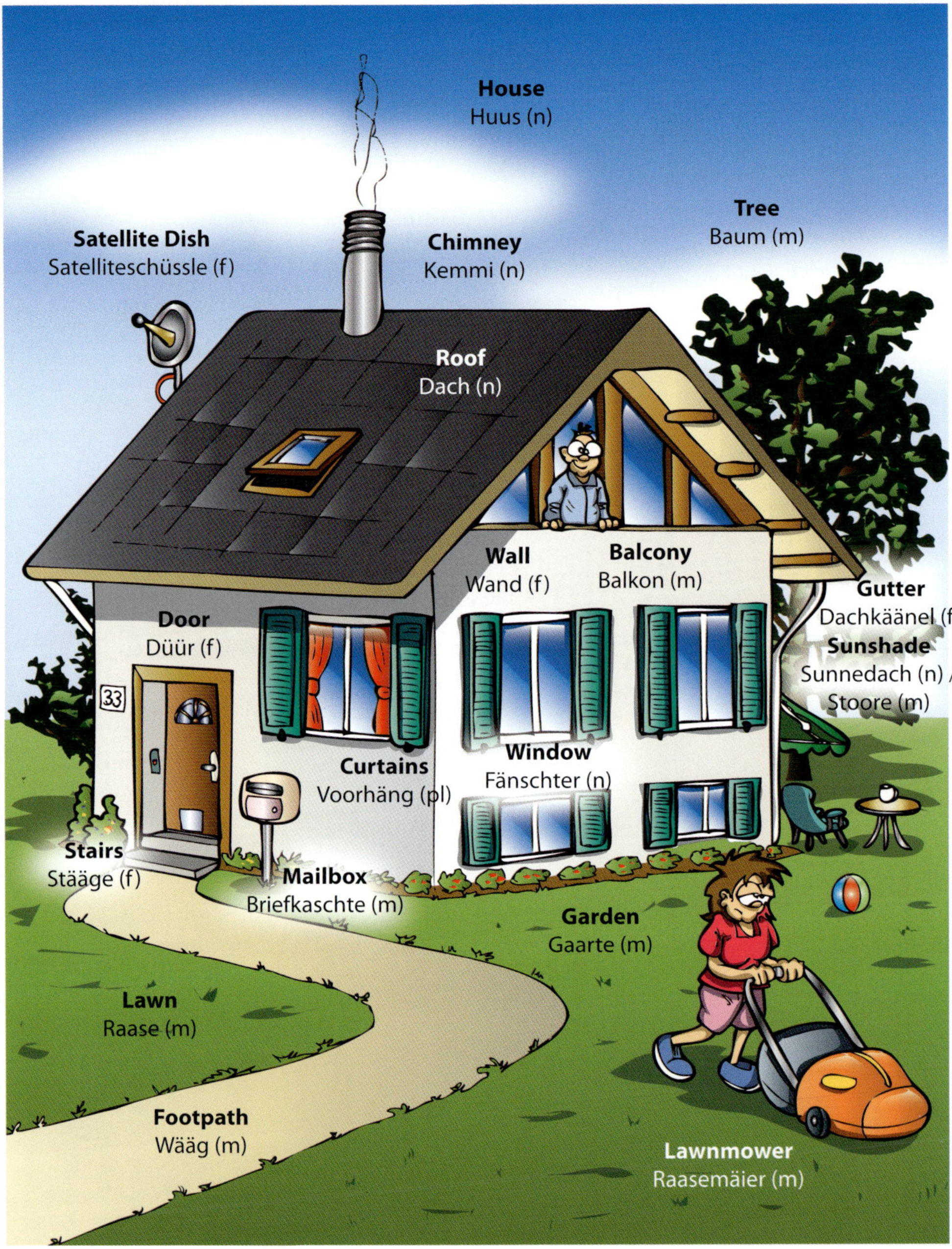

Housing

House Huus (n)
Satellite Dish Satelliteschüssle (f)
Chimney Kemmi (n)
Tree Baum (m)
Roof Dach (n)
Wall Wand (f)
Balcony Balkon (m)
Gutter Dachkäänel (f)
Door Düür (f)
Sunshade Sunnedach (n) / Stoore (m)
Curtains Voorhäng (pl)
Window Fänschter (n)
Stairs Stääge (f)
Mailbox Briefkaschte (m)
Garden Gaarte (m)
Lawn Raase (m)
Footpath Wääg (m)
Lawnmower Raasemäier (m)

Survival Kit

Parts of the house

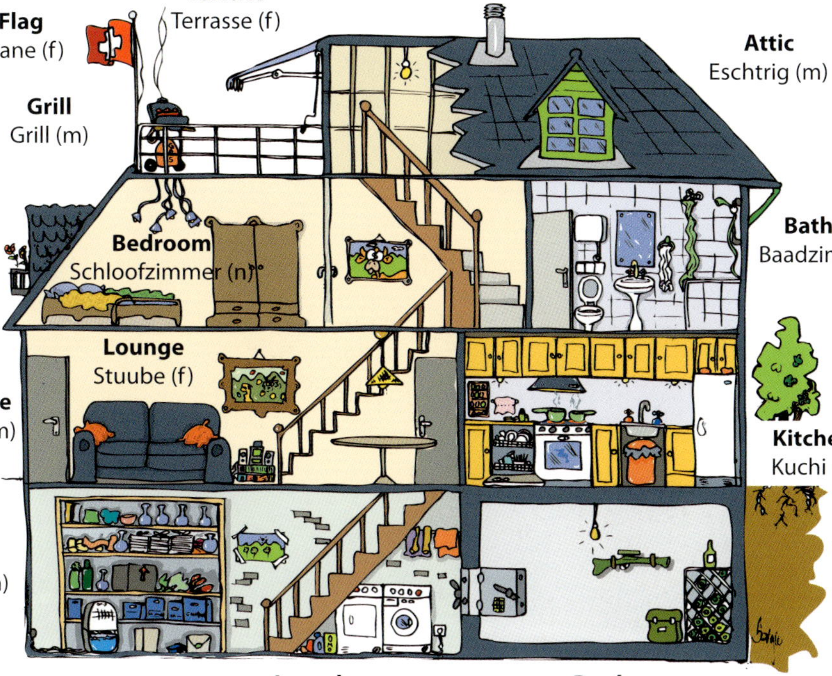

Flag — Faane (f)
Terrace — Terrasse (f)
Grill — Grill (m)
Attic — Eschtrig (m)
Bedroom — Schloofzimmer (n)
Bathroom — Baadzimmer (n)
Lounge — Stuube (f)
Entrance — Iigang (m)
Kitchen — Kuchi (f)
Cellar — Käller (m)
Laundry room — Wöschkuchi (f)
Bunker — Luftschutzkäller (m) / Bunker (m)

Housing

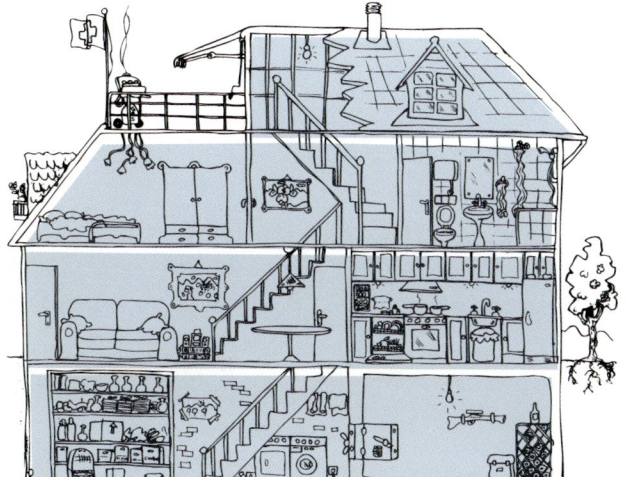

 Top floor — der oberschti Stock

 First floor — der erschti Stock

 Ground floor — Baarteer (n) *(franz.: parterre)*

 Basement — Käller (m)

Sali zämme - your Baseldütsch survival guide

Kitchen utensils

Bowl	Schüssle (f)	Jam jar	Gomfiglaas (n)
Box	Schachtle (f)	Kitchen cupboard	Kuchikäschtli (n)
	Kischte (f)	Knife	Mässer (n)
Chair	Stuel (m)	Microwave	Mikrowälle (f)
Cup	Dasse (f)	Napkin	Serviette (f)
Cutlery	Bstegg (n)	Oven	Baggoofe (m)
Dinner service	Gschirr (n) / Service (n)	Pan	Pfanne (f)
Dishes	Gschiir (n)	Plate	Däller (m)
Dishwasher	Abwäschmaschiine (f)	Rubbish bin	Mischtküübel (m)
Faucet / tap	Haane (m)	Spoon	Löffel (m)
Fork	Gaable (f)	Stove	Häärd (m)
Freezer	Diefkieler (m)	Table	Disch (m)
Fridge	Iiskaschte (m)	Table cloth	Dischduech (n)
Frying pan	Brootpfanne (f)	Table mats	Dischset (n)
Glass	Glaas (n)	Teaspoon	Teelöffeli (n)

Housing

Be Aware...
Zimmer refers to any other room than the kitchen or bathroom. So a **Zwäizimmerwoonig** is a flat with a living room and *one* bedroom, a kitchen and a bathroom.

Other house areas

		Garage	Garaasch (f) *(franz.: garage)*
Basement garage	Diefgaraasch (f) / Iistellhalle (f)	Hallway	Gang (m)
Building	Geböid (n)	Lobby	Iigangshalle (f) / Voorruum (m)
Children's room	Kinderzimmer (n)		
Dining room	Ässzimmer (n)	new building	Nöibau (m)
Entry way	Iigang (m)	old building	Altbau (m)
Floor	Boode (m)	Utility room	Abstellkämmerli (m)

Survival Kit

Toiletries

Bath tub	Baadwanne (f)
Body lotion	Köörpermilch (f)
Brush	Bürschte (f)
Comb	Strääl (m)
Deodorant	Deo (m)
Hand cream	Handgreeme (f)
Make-up	Schminkzüüg (n)
Mirror	Spiegel (m)
Razor blades	Rasierklinge (f)
Scales	Woog (f)
Shampoo	Schampo (n)
Shower	Duschi (f)
Shower cream	Duschmittel (n)
Shower curtain	Duschvoorhang (m)
Soap	Säiffi (f)
Toilet paper	Weezee-Papiir (WC-Papiir) (n)
Toiletries	Dualettesache (pl)
Toiletry bag	Nessesseer (n) *(franz.: nécessaire)*
Toothbrush	Zaanbürschtli (n)
Toothpaste	Zaanbaschta (f)
Towel	Diechli (n) / Wäschblätz (m)
Washbasin	Brünneli (n) / Lawaboo (n)

Housing

Other things in the house

Book shelves	Biechergstell (n)	**Key**	Schlüssel (m)
Carpet	Deppig (m)	**Pillow**	Küssi (n)
Closet	Kaschte (m)	**Plug**	Stegger (m)
Desk	Pult (n)	**Remote control**	Fäärnbedienig (f)
Doorbell	Huusglogge (f)	**Sheet**	Liinduech (n)
Drawer	Schuublaade (f)	**Tumble dryer**	Tömbler (m)
Duvet	Deggi (f)	**Wardrobe**	Gaarderoobe (f)
Hanger	Gläiderbüügel (m)	**Washing machine**	Wöschmaschiine (f)
Iron	Glettiise (n)		

Sali zämme - your Baseldütsch survival guide

Neighbours and agencies

Looking for a flat

Furnished room / furnished flat	möblierts Zimmer / möblierti Woonig (f)
Quiet area	rueigi Laag (f)
List of deficiencies	Mängellischte (f)
I am looking for a cheap flat.	Ich suech e günschtigi Woonig.
Is the flat quiet / big / sunny?	Isch d Woonig rueig / gross / sunnig?
Do you have a flat for rent?	Hänn Sii e Woonig zem Vermiete? (fr)
Do you know anybody who has a flat to rent?	Kenne Sii öpper, won e Woonig zem Vermiete hett? (fr)
	Kennsch (du) öpper, won e Woonig zem Vermiete hett? (inf)

Housing

Survival Kit

Laundry

Detergent	Wöschmittel (n)
Laundry basket	Wöschkorb (m) / Wöschzäine (f)
Laundry	Wösch (f)
Laundry bag	Wöschsagg (m)
Laundry day	Wöschdaag (m)
Laundry room	Wöschkuchi (f)
Laundry schedule	Wöschblaan (m)
to iron	glette
Tumble drier	Tömbler (m)
washing	wäsche
Washing machine	Wöschmaschiine (f)

TIP... Neighbours are usually quite friendly. You could engage in small talk using the different sections of this Survival Guide. Still, as it is common practice in Switzerland to share all the laundry facilities with them, in most cases the laundry room might be the only place you communicate with your neighbours.

Some housing words

Attic flat	Dachwoonig (f)
	Attikawoonig (f)
Estate agency	Verwaltig (f)
Home owner	Huusbsitzer (m)
	Huusbsitzere (f)
Landlord	Vermieter (m)
	Vermietere (f)
Neighbours	Noochbere (pl)
One-room flat	Äizimmerwoonig (f)
Rental flat	Mietwoonig (f)
Tenant	Mieter (m)
	Mietere (f)
Two-level flat	Mesonett-Woonig (f)
	(franz.: Maisonnette)
Flat with 2 rooms	Zwäizimmerwoonig (f)

Housing

Neighbourly survival phrases

Please close the door!	Bitte mache Sii d Huusdüür(e) zue!
Where can I deposit my rubbish?	Wo kaan ich der Abfall aanedue?
Could you please keep the noise down?	Könnte Sii bitte e bitz(li) rueig sii??
I'm trying to sleep.	Ich möcht schloofe.
Would you like to come over for a coffee?	Wänn Sii emoll ze uns zem Kaffi koo?
I'm your new neighbour.	Ich bi iire nöie Noochber. (m)
	Ich bi liri nöii Nochbere. (f)

Sali zämme - your Baseldütsch survival guide

Estate agent survival phrases (formal)

I have problems with my neighbours.	Ich ha Brobleem / Krach mit de Noochbere.
The... is not working.	Der ... isch kabutt. / Der ... isch hii.
Please, can you send a repairman?	Wurde Sii bitte e Handwärker verbiischigge?
When are we signing the contract?	Wenn kööne mer der Verdraag underschriibe?
I will move in, in...	Ich zie im ... ii.
I will move out in…	Ich zie im ... uss.
We need to check the inventory.	Mir mien no s Abnaam-Brotokoll mache.
It was like that when I moved in.	So hetts ussgsee, wo mir iizooge sinn.

Questions you may ask your landlord (formal)

How much is the rent?	Wie isch der Mietzins?
What services are included in the rent?	Was isch alles im Mietzins inbegriffe?
Do you have a cellar / attic /...?	Hets e Käller / en Eschtrig?
How much is a parking space per month?	Wie düür isch der Paarkblatz pro Moonet?
How long is the cancellation period?	Wie lang isch d Kündigungsfrischt?
Where can I do my laundry?	Wo kaa me d Wösch mache?
When can I do my laundry?	Wenn kaan ich wäsche?
Are pets allowed?	Sinn Huusdier erlaubt?
How much is the deposit?	Wie hooch isch d Kauzioon?
Is there a school / playground nearby?	Hetts e Schuelhuus / e Spiilblatz in der Nööchi?
Are you planning to raise the rent?	Hänn Sii im Sinn mit em Mietzins uffezgoo?
Can I paint the walls?	Kaan ich d Zimmer nöi striiche?
When was the house renovated?	Wenn isch das Huus renoviert woorde?
When can I move in?	Wenn kaan ich iizieh?
Can I use the terrace / garden?	Daarf ich d Terrasse / der Garte benutze?
How far is it to the next tram station?	Wie wit ischs bis zem Dramm / Drämmli?

Housing

Survival Kit

BE AWARE... In Switzerland the landlord will always ask for a confirmation that you have a good credit standing:

Kaan ich e Bedriibigsusszuug haa?
(May I have a clearance from the debt collection office?)

Housing

Questions your **landlord** may ask you (formal)

Are you married?	Sinn Sii ghüüroote?
Do you have pets?	Hänn Sii Huusdier?
Yes, I have a dog / guinea pig.	Joo, ich haan e Hund / e Meersöili.
Do you have a steady income?	Hänn Sii e reegelmäässigs Iikomme?
How much do you earn?	Wie viil verdiene Sii?
I earn … francs.	Ich verdien … Frangge.
Do you have any children?	Hänn Sii Kinder?
How old are they?	Wie alt sinn si?
Do you play an instrument?	Spiile Sii en Inschtrumänt?
Do you party a lot?	Dien Sii viil feschte?
Are you a foreigner?	Sinn Sii Ussländer? / Sinn Sii Ussländere?
Where are you from?	Vo wo kömme Sii?
Have you ever been prosecuted?	Sinn Sii jee bedriibe woorde?
Do you smoke?	Rauche Sii?
Yes, I smoke.	Joo, ich rauch.
No, I don't smoke.	Näi, ich rauch nit.

Sali zämme - your Baseldütsch survival guide

Numbers

Be Aware... In Baseldütsch, as in High German, digits are called **Zaale**. Number is **Nummere** and refers to a set of digits, e.g. **Delifonnummere** (phone number) or **Huusnummere** (house number).

Ordinal numbers

ten	zää
eleven	elf
twelve	zwölf
thirteen	drizää
fourteen	vierzää
fifteen	fuffzää
sixteen	sächzää
seventeen	sibzää
eighteen	achzää
nineteen	nüünzää
twenty	zwanzig
thirty	drissig
forty	vierzig
fifty	fuffzig
sixty	sächzig
seventy	sibzig
eighty	achzig
ninety	nüünzig
one hundred	hundert

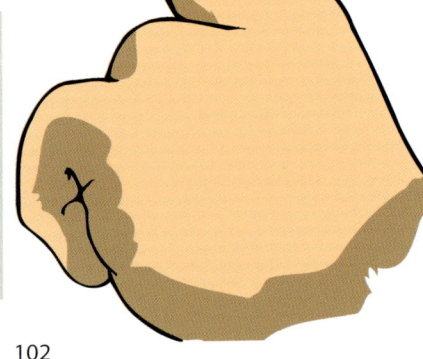

- äins **1**
- zwäi **2**
- drei **3**
- vier **4**
- fümf **5**
- säggs **6**
- siibe **7**
- acht **8**
- nüün **9**
- Stäärn(m) / Stäärnli (n) *****
- null **0**
- Doppelgrüzz / Gaartehaag **#**

Ordinal numbers

two hundred	zwäihundert
one thousand	dausig / duusig
two thousand	zwäidausig / zwäiduusig
hundred thousand	hundertdausig / hundertduusig
one million	e Million (f)
one billion	e Milliarde (f)

Miscellaneous

Survival Kit

Cardinal numbers

first	erscht	sixth	säggst
second	zwäit	seventh	sibt
third	dritt	eighth	acht
fourth	viert	ninth	nüünt
fifth	fümft	tenth	zäänt

Other numbers

Code	Ghäimnummere (f)
	Kood (m) /Pinnkood
equals	git / isch gliich
even numbers	graadi Zaale
House number	Huusnummere (f)
Insurance number	Versicherigsnummere (f)
lucky number	Glüggszaal (f)
minus	minus
odd numbers	ungraadi Zaale
Pension number	Aahaavau-Nummere (AHV-Nummere) (f)
Phone number	Delifonnummere (f)
plus	und / plus
unlucky number	Unglüggszaal (f)

Miscellaneous

Sali zämme - your Baseldütsch survival guide

Toilets

Public toilet words

engaged/ occupied	bsetzt	**Toilet paper**	Weezee-Papiir / Dualette-Papiir (n)
Hand dryer	Händedroggner (m)	**Urinal**	Pissuar (n) *(franz.: Pissoir)*
Paper towel	Bapiirhandtuech (n)	**vacant**	frei
Soap	Säiffi (f)	**Washbasin**	Lawaboo (n) / Brünneli (n)
Toilet	Dualette (f) *(franz.: Toilette)* Weezee (n)		

Miscellaneous

Key survival phrases

Where is the toilet?	Wo isch s Weezee (n)?
	Wo isch d Dualette (f)? *(franz.: Toilette)*
	Wo isch s Hüüsli?
May I use your toilet?	Kaan i rasch uff d Dualette / uff s Weezee? / uffs Hüüsli?
Men's toilet	Männerweezee / Herredualette (pl)
Women's toilet	Fraueweezee / Daamedualette (pl)
Do you have any toilet paper?	Hänn Sii Weezee-Papiir / Dualette-Papiir? (fr)
	Hesch (du) Weezee-Papiir / Dualette-Papiir? (inf)
Where is the toilet light?	Wo ischs Weezee-Liecht / dr Weezee-Schalter?
What is the code to open the toilet door?	Wie isch der Kood für d Dualette / fürs Weezee?

Survival Kit

Education

BE AWARE... Beginning of summer holidays: **"Bündelidaag"** (probably the most important day for children...)

Key survival words

Baccalaureate	Maduur (f)	**recess / break**	Pause (f)
biro / pen	Kulli (m)	**rubber / eraser**	Gummi (m)
book	Buech (m)	**school bag**	Schuelsagg (m) / Ruggsagg (m)
day care	Krippe (f)		
exam	Briefig (f) / Schriftligi (f)	**school report**	Züügnis (n)
fountain pen	Fülli (n)	**teacher**	Leerer (m)
Gymnasium	Gimnaasium / Gimmeli (n)		Leerere (f)
high school	Sekundaarschuel / Sek (f)	**test**	Tescht (m)
homework	Uffgoobe / Huus-Uffgoobe (pl)	**to cheat**	bschisse
		to cheat	spigge / abluege
kindergarten	Kindsgi (m) / Hääfelischuel (m)	**to cram / to drill**	büffle / oggse / schanze
		to learn	leere
pencil	Bleistift (m)	**to teach**	leere
primary school	Brimaarschuel / Brimmeli (f)	**university**	Uni / Universideet (f)
		writing utensils	Schriibzüüg (n)

General non-specific terms

Generic words

anything	irgendöppis
nothing	nüt
somebody	öpper
somehow	irgendwie
something	öppis
sometimes	männgmool / männgisch / albe / öppe / öppedie / amme
somewhere	nöime / näime
thing	Sach (f)
	Ding (n)

Measurements

long	lang
large	gross
medium	mittel / mittelgross
short	kurz / gläi
wide	wiit
big	gross
small	gläi

Miscellaneous

TIP... 'z' means 'too' in English and can be used with lots of adjectives:

z viil	too much/many
z weenig	too few / too little
z frie	too early
z spoot	too late
z lang	too long

Time

early	frie
in a moment	graad / glii
late	spoot
moment	Momänt (m)
now	jetz
soon	glii / bald

Quantity

a pair	e baar (weenigi) veräinzelti
few	weenig
less / fewer	weeniger
more	mee
much / many	viil
some	äinigi
too many	z viil
too much	z viil

Survival Kit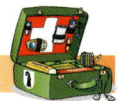

Colours

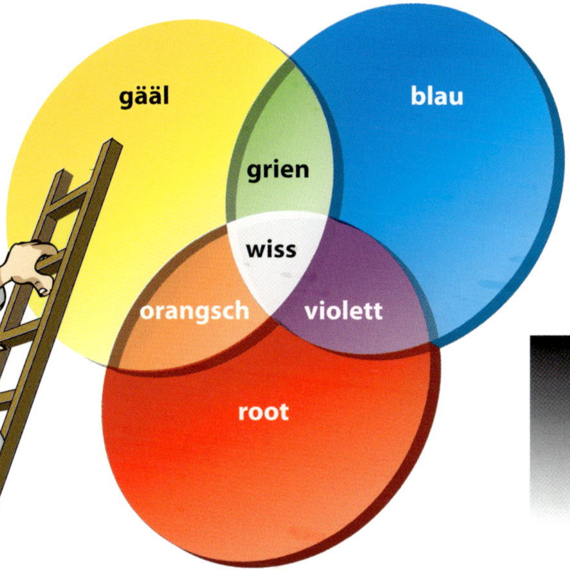

gääl · **blau** · **grien** · **wiss** · **orangsch** · **violett** · **root**

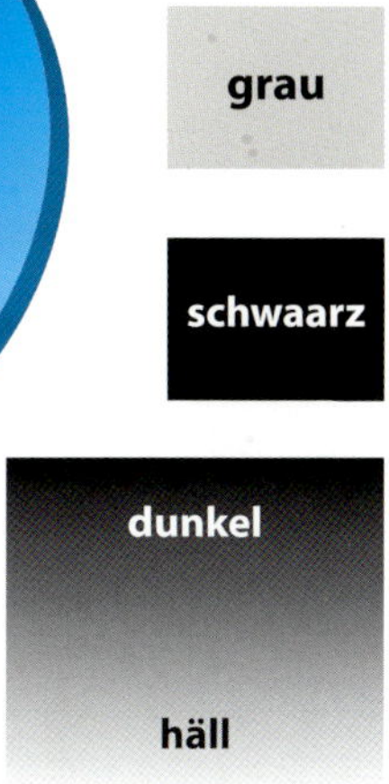

grau · **schwaarz** · **dunkel** · **häll**

Other colours

pink	roosa	**brown**	bruun
silver	silbrig	**beige**	beesch
gold	goldig	**lilac**	lila

Expressions related to colours

Baseldütsch Idiom	Meaning	Literal translation
grien hinder den Oore	immature	green behind the ears
e griene Duume	to be good with plants	to have a green thumb
schwaarz (g)see	to be pessimistic	to see it black
Schwaarzmäärt (m)	illegal market	Black market
e goldigi Hand	a lucky hand	a golden hand
e wissi Weschde	innocent	A white waistcoat / vest
blau / er isch blau	to be drunk	to be 'blue'
e graui Muus	a person that no one notices	A grey mouse
dur e roosarooti Brülle luege	to be naïve / overly optimistic	to see things through pink glasses

Miscellaneous

Sali zämme - your Baseldütsch survival guide

Animals

Bird Voogel (m)

Fish Fisch (m)

Songbird Singvoogel (m) *(at Fasnacht only)*

Fly Fliege (f)

European ibex Stäibogg (m)

Horse Ross (n)

Cow Kue (f)

Pig Sau (f)

Chicken Huen (n)

Cat Katz, Buusle (f) Kaater, Maudi (m) Buusi (n)

Snake Schlange (f)

Rabbit Küngel (m)

Dog Hund (m)

Miscellaneous

Alpine wildlife

Buzzard	Möisebussard (m)	**Marmot**	Muurmeli (n)
Chamois	Gams, Gäms (f) / Gämsi (n)		Muurmeldier (n)
Deer	Hirsch (m)		Mungg (n)
Eagle	Aadler (m)	**Marten**	Maarder (m)
Goat	Gäiss (f)	**Mouse**	Muus (f) / Müüsli (n)
Fox	Fuggs (m)	**Roe deer**	Ree (n)
Jackdaw	Doole (f)	**Wild boar**	Wildsau (f)
Lynx	Luggs (m)	**Wolf**	Wolf (m)

Survival Kit

Other animals

Bear	Bäär (m)	Hippopotamus	Niilpfäärd (n)
Bull	Stier (m)		Flusspfäärd (n)
Crocodile	Groggedill (n)	Lamb	Lamm (n)
Donkey	Eesel (m)	Lion	Löi (m)
Elephant	Elefant (m)	Lizard	Äideggse (f) /
Guinea pig	Meersöili (n)		Äideggsli (n)
		Monkey	Aff (m)

Rhinoceros	Naashorn (n)
Rooster	Güggel (m)
Tiger	Diiger (m)
Turtle	Schildgrot (f)
Zebra	Zeebra (n)

Warning!! Hungry Bears beyond this point

Miscellaneous

Bugs / Insects

Ant	Aamäise (f)	Insect	Inseggt (n)
Bee	Biene (f) / Bienli (n)	Mosquito	Mugge (f)
Beetle	Kääfer (m)	Slug	Schnägg (m)
Bug	Wäntele (f)	Spider	Spinne (f)
Cockroach	Schwoobekääfer (f)	Wasp	Wäschbi (n)
Fly	Fliege (f)	Worm	Wuurm (m)

Sali zämme - your Baseldütsch survival guide

Time

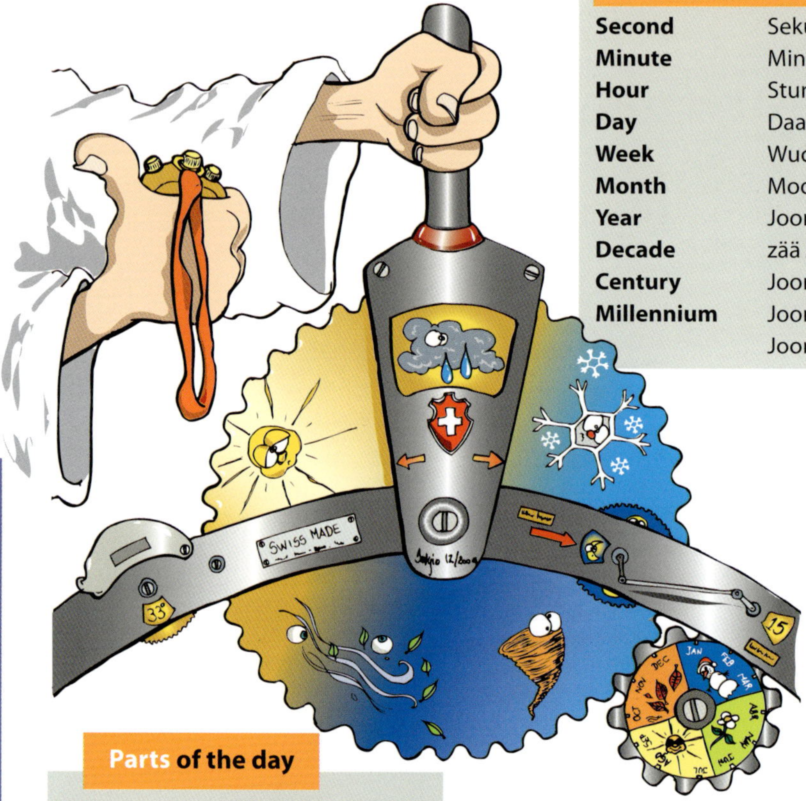

Time measurements

Second	Sekunde (f)
Minute	Minute (f)
Hour	Stund (f)
Day	Daag (m)
Week	Wuche (f)
Month	Moonet (m)
Year	Joor (n)
Decade	zää Joor (f)
Century	Joorhundert (n)
Millennium	Joordausig / Joorduusig (n)

Parts of the day

Dawn	Dämmerig (f)
	Moorgedämmerig (f)
Morning	Moorge (m)
Noon / Midday	Mittag (m)
Afternoon	Noomidaag (m)
Evening	Oobe (m)
Dusk	Dämmerig (f)
	Oobedämmerig (f)
Night	Nacht (f)
Midnight	Mitternacht
Four a.m. *(at Fasnacht)*	Morgestraich

TIP... The answer to the question 'when' is **'am'** for masculine and **'in der'** for feminine nouns: **am Mittag** (at noon), **in der Nacht** (at night).

Survival Kit

Moments in time

Past	verbii / umme / vergange Vergangehäit (f)
Present / now	jetz / im Momänt / momäntaan / zer Zit Geegewaart (f)
Future	Zuekumft (f) zuekümftig / in Zuekumft
Yesterday	geschter
Today	hütt(e)
Tomorrow	moorn
Weekend	Wuchenänd (n)
the day before yesterday	voorgeschter
the day after tomorrow	üübermoorn

Key survival phrases

What time is it?	Was isch für Zit? / Wie spoot isch es?
At what time ...?	Wenn ...?
When do we meet?	Wenn dräffe mer is?
	Wenn wämmer is dräffe?
When do you go to ...?	Wenn göön Sii uff ...? (fr)
	Wenn goosch (du) uff ...? (inf)
Sorry, I am late.	Duet mer läid, ich bi z spoot.
I will be 10 minutes late.	Ich kumm zää Minute spööter.
What day is today?	Was hämmer hütt für e Daag?
	Was isch hütt für e Daag?
When is that?	Wenn isch das?
From when / until when?	Vo wenn / bis wenn?
exactly	genau
Do you have time?	Hänn Sii e Momänt Zit? (fr)
	Hesch (du) e Momänt Zit? (inf)
every week	all Wuche / jeedi Wuche
every year	all Joor / jeedes Joor
When does the film start?	Wenn fangt der Film aa?
When does the film finish?	Wenn isch der Film feertig?
How long does the film last?	Wie lang goot der Film?
The film starts at ...	Der Film fangt am ... aa.
The film finishes at ...	Der Film höört am ... uff.
Be on time!	Sig pünggtlig!

Miscellaneous

Sali zämme - your Baseldütsch survival guide

Months

January	Januaar (m)
February	Februaar (m)
March	Meerz (m)
April	April (m)
May	Mäi (m)
June	Juni (m)
July	Juli (m)
August	Auguscht (m)
September	Septämber (m)
October	Oggtoober (m)
November	Novämber (m)
December	Dezämber (m)

Days of the week

Monday	Määntig
Tuesday	Zischtig
Wednesday	Mittwuch
Thursday	Donnschtig
Friday	Fritig
Saturday	Samschtig
Sunday	Sunntig

Seasons

Season	Jooreszit (f)
Spring	Frielig (m)
Summer	Summer (m)
Autumn	Herbscht (m)
Winter	Winter (m)

Miscellaneous

TIP... Although most people have a watch, sometimes you will be asked: **Hänn Sii en Uur?** (Do you have a watch?). This question means: What time is it?

TIP... All the months, days of the week and the seasons are masculine, which means that **'der'** is used: **der Januar, der Määntig, der Frielig.**

Survival Kit

Telling time

säggsi	fümf ab säggsi	zää ab säggsi	Viertel ab säggsi	zwanzig ab säggsi

fümf voor halber siibeni *(literally: five before half seven)*	halber siibeni	fümf ab halber siibeni *(literally: five after half seven)*

zwanzig voor siibeni	Viertel voor siibeni	zää voor siibeni	fümf voor siibeni	siibeni

TIP... To indicate time, the preposition 'am' is used: **am drei** means at three, **am säggsi** means at 6 o'clock.

Before — voor | ab — After

Sali zämme - your Baseldütsch survival guide

Weather and temperature

Be Aware... The 'weather verbs' (**räägne, schneie**, etc.) always need the impersonal subject **es** or **s**: **(e)s räägnet** (it's raining).

Key survival phrases

The sun is shining.	D Sunne schiint.
It's raining.	Es räägnet.
It's snowing.	Es schneit.
It's chilly/foggy/humid.	S isch früsch / nääblig / fiecht.
It's going to rain.	S kunnt ko räägne / schiffe.
Today it's very warm / cold.	Hütt ischs seer waarm / kalt.
It's getting chilly.	S wird früsch.
Summer is coming.	Der Summer kunnt.
The weather is improving.	S duet uff.
warm wind coming from the south	Föön (m)
What is the weather forecast for tomorrow?	Wie isch der Wätterbricht für moorn?
	Was säit der Wätterbricht für moorn?

Miscellaneous

Survival Kit

Weather and temperature

Climate	Kliima (n)	**Lightning**	Blitz (m)
cloudy	bewölkt / bedeggt	**Rain**	Rääge (m) / räägne
sunny	sunnig	**Snow**	Schnee (m)
cold	kalt	**Storm**	Stuurm (m)
cool	früsch / kiel	**Sun**	Sunne (f)
dry	drogge	**Temperature**	Temperatuur (f)
Fog	Nääbel (m)	**Thunder**	Donner (m)
Forecast	Wätterbricht (m)	**Thunderstorm**	Gwitter (n)
Hail	Haagel (m) / haagle	warm	waarm
Heat	Hitz (f)	**Weather**	Wätter (n)
hot	häiss	**Weather report**	Wätterbricht (m)
humid	fiecht	**Wind**	Wind (m)

Miscellaneous

Decoding the Swiss

Part III

Decoding the Basler

Sali zämme - your Baseldütsch survival guide

Slang words in Baseldütsch

This last part of the Survival Guide presents some Baseldütsch words and expressions that are often used in an informal environment. People of all social classes and ages use some of them, but it is the younger generation that may be found speaking this 'slanguage' more often.

The origin of Basel's 'slanguage' varies; some words are typical Swiss words that have adopted a new meaning, metaphorical in some cases (**D Uffzgi sinn schoggi** – Homework is easy). Some other words originate from a foreign language but the grammatical pattern follows a Swiss German one. In particular the influence of American and British culture, which is quite strong, plays an important role in younger people's words and expressions (e.g. **fuude** for to eat).

Decoding the Swiss

Slang words in Baseldütsch

A

abdanze	to dance non-stop
äin schnappe	to drink
äin zie	to drink
äinewääg	in any event / anyway
aakotze	to be reluctant to do something
aaschisse	not in the mood for something
Buff (n)	disorder
Bulver (m)	money
Buschi	Baby
Buschiwaage	pram / stroller
büügle	to work hard

B

Baabe (f)	doltish woman
bache	to sleep
Baiz (f)	restaurant, pub
Bebbi (m)	name 'Jacob'; a man from Basel
Blausch (m)	lots of fun
bleegere	to relax
böimig	great, brilliant

D

Daig (m)	dough; the long established, wealthy Basel families
Dasch der Hammer!	super!
Depp (m)	dimwit
dervooseggle	to run away

Continued on the next page..

119

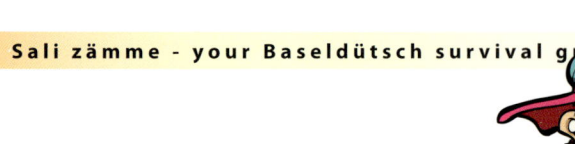

Sali zämme - your Baseldütsch survival g

Slang words in Baseldütsch

dervoozäpfe	to run away
Ditti, Ditteli (n)	doll
Do isch öppis loos gsii.	It was exciting/ lots of fun
Donne (f)	1000 Swiss francs
Düpfi (f)	featherbrained woman
Düpflischisser (m)	fusspot
Duubel (m)	nitwit

E
e Knall haa	crazy
ebe	that's what I said, exactly
en Abgang mache	to leave

F
Faggel (m)	note, a slip of paper
Friise (f)	hairstyle
Frosch (m)	cigarette
fuetere	to eat something

G
Gäggsnaase (f)	smart aleck woman
gäil	very cool
gediige	comfortable
gfelligscht	please (angrily said)
gruusig	bad, disgusting
Gugge (f)	(paper) bag
Gumsle (f)	obnoxious / irritating women
Guttere (f)	a bottle
güügele	to drink

H
häilloos	extremely
heerlig	peaceful/ comfortable
horränd	extremely

I
iinebiige	to eat something

J
jääsele	to stink

Decoding the Swiss

Slang words in Baseldütsch

K
käi Aanig	no idea
Kätzli (f)	attractive woman
Kiis (n)	money
Kischte (f)	a million francs
klaue	to steal
kuul	cool

L
Labbe (m)	100 francs
Lungebröötli (n)	cigarette

M
mämmele	to drink
mampfe	to eat something
männg / männgs	a lot of something
mega	extremely, super
müffele	to have a bad odour

P
Pfiffe (m)	useless, incompetent person
pfuuse	to sleep/to take a nap

S
Saggladäärne (n)	torch
sau	very, extremely
sauguet	remarkably good
schampaar	extremely
schief	odd, strange
Schloot (n)	heavy smoker
schloote	to smoke heavily
Schmiir (m)	police
Schnitte (f)	attractive woman
Schnüggel (m)	nice looking guy
Schnuure (f)	mouth (often too big)
schreeg	odd, strange
Schooffseggel	dimwit
schwoofe	to dance
simsle	to send an SMS to someone
sputte	to eat something
Stutz (m)	money
Suchthuffe (m)	person with obsessive behaviour
suffe	to drink a lot
super	great, brilliant

T
tschegge	to understand
Tschumpel	blockhead

U
ummehange	to spend time somewhere or with someone

V
veraarsche	to cheat on somebody
verhäize	to mistreat
verhaue	to fail (a test)
verreggt	extremely
verruggt	extremely
versieche	to fail (a test)

W
Wäisch wie!	Really great, isn't it?
Was goot do ab?	What's up?

Z
Zämme!	Hi, guys !
zem Vergässe	to forget, to fail
zie	have a drink
Zwuggel (m)	small person; small child

Sali zämme - your Baseldütsch survival guide

Swiss idioms in Baseldütsch

Sayings and expressions are a key part of the linguistic heritage of a society. They are very interesting since they reflect, in a playful way, a lot about the social culture, and the Swiss are quite creative when it comes to using them.

As a final point, we would like to introduce some idiomatic sayings and expressions in Baseldütsch. The majority of these are unique to Baseldütsch and Swiss German.

Decoding the Swiss

Basel idiom	Literal translation	Meaning
Er isch ussgraschtet.	He freaked out.	He freaked out.
Sii hett e langi Läitig.	She has a long cable.	She is slow to catch the meaning.
uffs Grootwool	on the off chance	With a bit of luck
Doo ligt der Hund begraabe.	That's where the dog is buried.	the crux of the matter
Das isch käi Hoonigschlägge.	It's not a honey lick.	It's difficult.
nit alli Dasse im Schrank	not all cups in the cupboard / S/he's missing cups in his/her cupboard.	crazy / not too clever.
Sii isch blauöigig.	She is blue-eyed.	She is naive.
Das isch käi Schlägg.	That's not a lick.	It's difficult.
s Hinderletschti	The last thing.	last thing possible / the worst thing
Er kennt nüt.	He doesn't know anything.	He goes for it despite the odds.
Sii hett alles gää.	She gave everything.	She put in a maximum of effort.
Er isch schaarf uff sii.	He is hot on her.	He fancies her (sexually).
vo Tuute und Bloose käi Aanig	no idea about hooting nor blowing	Really naïve / uninformed
ufflääse	to scrape up	to pick up
e spitzi Zunge	A pointed tongue	straight to the point / with criticism
Er hett sii abgschlebbt.	He towed her off.	He persuaded her to go home with him

Sali zämme - your Baseldütsch survival guide

Basel idiom	Literal translation	Meaning
Hesch e Schuss?	Do you have a bang?	Are you crazy?
Bisch duure bi root?	Have you crossed on the red?	Have you lost your mind?
Äins ums ander wie z Pariis.	One thing after another, just like in Paris	one thing after another
e Sprung in der Schüssle	a crack in the bowl	crazy
Goots no?	No way!	For sure not!
Ammene gschänggte Gaul luegt me nit ins Muul.	Don't look a gift horse in the mouth.	If it's a gift, don't criticize it.

Basel idiom	Literal translation	Meaning
uffgläise	to rerail	to initiate / implement something
Ich drugg dir der Duume.	I press my thumb for you.	I'm crossing my fingers for you / wish you good luck.
Dä kaa mir der Buggel aaberutsche.	He can slide down my hump.	He can go jump in a lake.
Sii macht käi Wangg.	She doesn't move.	She doesn't move or make a sound.
Hans was Häiri.	John is like Henry.	It's all the same.
Er macht d Fuscht im Sagg.	He puts his fist in his pocket.	He is hiding how furious he is.
Glöpfer-Promi / Servela-Promi	sausage VIP starlet	a would-like-to-be famous person
Schiggi-Miggi	chic person	posh person
Sii heebe zämme wie Bäch und Schwääfel.	They stick together like pitch and sulphur.	They are inseparable friends.
Er faart voll uf daas ab.	He drives completely after this.	He is very enthusiastic about this.
Sii wott der Batze und s Weggli.	She wants the penny and the roll.	She wants to keep her cake and eat it too.
Er schwimmt im Gäld.	He is swimming in money.	He is very rich.
grampfe wien e Duubel	work like a madman	to work a lot/ to struggle
e Katzesprung	only a cat jump	Not far from here.
Jetz kumm i druss.	I'm coming out.	Now I understand.
lamaaschig	just like a lama	very slow

Sali zämme - your Baseldütsch survival guide

Frequent confusions

When Swiss people speak High German you can usually immediately recognise them as being Swiss because of their accent and the way they construct their sentences. And of course there is their special vocabulary. In 'Helvetic' High German dialect words are often just transferred into a German form. This means there are three versions: Swiss German, Helvetic German and Standard (High) German. On the following pages you'll find some words that will either cause confusion or amusement in Germany.

IS EVERYTHING CLEAR...?

	Confusing words		
English	**High German**	**in using High German a Swiss will say ... (Helvetic German)**	**Baseldütsch**
address	Anschrift	Adresse	Adrässe
agenda item	Tagesordnungspunkt	Traktandum	Traktandum (n)
appear (verb)	den Anschein haben	Den Anschein machen	der Aaschiin mache
attic	Dachstock (m)	Estrich	Eschtrig (m)
bag for toiletries	Kulturbeutel	Necessaire	Nessesseer (n) *(franz.: nécessaire)*
beet	Rote Beete	Randen	Rande (m)
bicycle	Fahrrad	Velo	Welo (n)
blond highlights	Blonde Strähnchen	Mèches	Meesch (pl) *(franz.: Mèches)*
blow (verb)	wehen	winden	winde
breakfast	Frühstück	Morgenessen	Zmoorge (m)

Decoding the Swiss

Confusing words

building super-intendent	Hausmeister	Abwart	Abwaart (m)
carpet	Teppichboden	Spannteppich	Spanndeppig (m)
carrot	Karotte	Rübli	Riebli
closet	Schrank	Kasten	Kaschte (m)
conductor	Schaffner	Kondukteur	Kondüggtöör (m) *(franz.: conducteur)*
contemplate (verb)	nachdenken	studieren	studiere
courgette	Zucchini	Zuchetti	Zuggetti (f)
crate for drinks	Getränkekiste	Harass	Haarasse (f)
cream	Sahne	Rahm	Raam (m)
debt collection	Schuldeneintreibung	Betreibung	Betriibig (f)
deposit	Pfand	Depot	Debbo (n) *(franz.: Depot)*
desk	Schreibtisch	Pult	Pult (n)
die (verb)	sterben	abserbeln	absäärble
driver	Fahrer	Chauffeur	Schofföör (m) *(franz.: Chauffeur)*
evening meal	Abendessen	Znachtessen	Znachtässe
fireplace	Kamin	Cheminée	Schminee (n) *(franz.: Cheminée)*
funeral service	Trauerfeier	Abdankung	Abdankig (f)
get rid of (verb)	loswerden	abschieben	abschiebe
get undressed (verb)	sich ausziehen / sich auskleiden	sich abziehen	sich abzie
go out (verb)	ausgehen / abends weggehen	in den Ausgang gehen	in Ussgang goo
go shopping (verb)	einkaufen / shoppen	lädeln	läädele
grapefruit	Pampelmuse (f)	Grapefrutt	Greipfrutt (f) *(engl.: Grapefruit)*
grill (verb)	grillen	grillieren	grilliere
hairdresser	Friseur	Coiffeur	Guafföör (m) *(franz.: Coiffeur)*
handkerchief	Taschentuch	Nastuch	Naasdiechli (n)
helicopter	Hubschrauber	Helikopter	Heli (m)
hen	Huhn	Poulet	Pulle (n) *(franz.: Poulet)*
hospital	Krankenhaus	Spital	Spidaal (m)
ice cream	Eis	Glacé	Glasse (f) *(franc.: Glace)*
ID	Personalausweis	Identitätskarte (ID)	Ii-Dee (ID) (f)
insinuate (verb)	andeuten	antönen	aadööne
interruption	Unterbrechung	Unterbruch	Underbruch (m)
iron (verb)	bügeln	glätten	glette
lamb's lettuce	Feldsalat	Nüsslisalat	Nüsslisalaat (m)
lorry / truck	Lastwagen	Camion	Laschtwaage (f)
mailman	Postbote	Pöstler	Böschtler (m)

Sali zämme - your Baseldütsch survival guide

Confusing words

English	German	Swiss German	Baseldütsch
make an appointment (verb)	sich verabreden	abmachen	abmache
mascara	Wimperntusche	Mascara	Maskara (f)
mess	Unordnung	nicht aufgeräumt	Buff (n)
motorcycle	Motorrad	Töff	Döff (m)
move house (verb)	umziehen	zügeln	züügle
on the other hand	andererseits	handkehrum	handkeerum
pant's fly	Hosenschlitz	Hosenladen	Hooselaade (m)
paprika	Paprika	Peperoni	Peperooni (f)
park (verb)	parken	parkieren	parkiere
parking ticket	Strafzettel	Busse	Buess (f)
pavement / sidewalk	Gehsteig	Trottoir	Trottuaar (n) *(franz.: Trottoir)*
peanuts	Erdnüsse	Spanische Nüsse	spanischi Nüssli
penthouse / loft	Penthouse	Attikawohnung	Attikawoonig (f)
perch	Barsch	Egli	Eegli (m)
perfect	perfekt	pico bello	piggo bello *(ital.: pico bello)*
plastic folder	Aktenhülle	Sichtmäppchen	Sichtmäppli (n)
platform / track	Bahnsteig	Perron	Perron (n)
pocket knife	Taschenmesser	Sackmesser	Saggmässer (m)
possibly	etwaig	allfällig	allfellig
proposition	Angebot	Offerte	Offärte (f)
purse / wallet	Geldbeutel	Portmonee	Bortmenee (n)
ring (verb)	klingeln	läuten	lütte
rustic	urig	urchig	urchig
scooter (with motor)	Roller	Vespa	Wespa(f)
scooter (no motor)	Tretroller	Trotinett	Trotinett (n)
secondhand shop	Gebrauchtwarenladen	Brokenhaus	Broggehuus (n)
service / tip	Bedienung	Service	Serwiss *(franz.: Service)*
shoestring	Schnürsenkel	Schuhbändel	Schuebändel (pl)
sit down (verb)	sich setzen	absitzen	absitze
ski boot	Skistiefel	Skischuhe	Schiischue (m)
skirt	Rock (m)	Jupe	Schüpp (m) *(franz.: Jupe)*
slippers	Hausschuhe	Finken	Fingge (m)
soon	innerhalb des Zeitrahmens	innert nützlicher Frist	innert nützliger Frischt
sound (verb)	klingen	tönen	dööne
spicy hot	scharf (gewürzt)	rassig	rassig
stapler	Tacker	Bostitch	Bostidsch (m) *(engl.: Bostitch)*
stationer's	Schreibwarengeschäft	Papeterie	Babbedderii (f) *(franz.: papeterie)*

Decoding the Swiss

Confusing words

strong-flavoured	würzig (Käse)	rezent	rezänt
suit jacket	Sakko / Anzugsjacke	Tschoppen	Kittel (m)
tabletop soccer	Tischfussball spielen	töggeln	döggele
telephone (verb)	anrufen	ein Telefon geben	e Delifoon gää
telephone (verb)	anrufen	anläuten	alütte
there is	es gibt	es hat	es het
ticket	Fahrkarte (f)	Billet	Billjee (n)
toboggan / sled	rodeln	schlitteln	schlittle
touch (verb)	berühren	anlangen	aalänge
tough	zäh (metaphorisch benutzt)	harzig	haarzig
traffic light	Verkehrsampel	Lichtsignal	Signaal / Liechtsignaal (n)
tram / streetcar	Strassenbahn	Tram	Dram / Drämmli (n)
tuna	Thunfisch	Thon	Thon (m)
vest	Weste	Gilet	Schile (n) *(franz.: Gilet)*
vote (verb)	seine Stimme abgeben/ wählen	stimmen / wählen	stimme / wääle
walnut	Walnuss	Baumnuss	Baumnuss (f)
washbasin	Waschbecken	Lavabo	Lawaboo (n)
wipe (verb)	kehren	wischen	wüsche
with the naked eye	mit blossem Auge	von Auge	vo Aug
within	innerhalb von (Zeitspanne)	innert	innert
work (verb)	arbeiten	schaffen	schaffe

 **Be Aware...** Baseldütsch can be very precise. For example, there are many different words for 'work':

grampfe / knüttle / meche / oggse / biggle	to slave away at something
schaffe / büügle	to work very hard
gfätterle / schäffele	to work a bit
hienere	to do something without thinking, to scat
pfusche / schluudere / höie	to goof around, to make stupid mistakes
künngele	to trifle, to take unnecessary time
döggterle / kiechle	to mess around, to go overboard in details
juufle	to work hastily, to rush
ummelauere	to idle, lazily take time

129

Appendix

Appendix

Sali zämme - your Baseldütsch survival guide

Pronouns and articles

Personal pronouns

	1st Person	2nd Person	3rd Person
nominative singular	iich / ich / i	duu /du	äär / er
accusative singular	mii /mi	dii / di	iin
dative singular	miir / mir	diir /dir / dr	iim
nominative plural	mir	iir /diir	sii
accusative plural	uns	öich	sii
dative plural	uns	öich	iine

Definite articles

	masculine	feminine	neuter	plural
common case	der / dr	d	s	d
dative case	am /em	dr	em	de

Indefinite articles

	masculine	feminine	neuter
common case	e	e	e
dative case	amme(ne)	anere	amme(ne)

Appendix

Demonstrative pronouns

	masculine	feminine	neuter	plural
common case	dää sälle	die sälli	daas säll	die sälli
dative case	däm sällem	dääre sällere	däm sällem	dääne sälle

Possessive pronouns

	masculine	feminine	neuter	plural
common case	mi	mi	mi	miini
dative case	mim	minere	mim	miine
common case	di	di	di	diini
dative case	dim	dinere	dim	diine
common case	si	si	si	siini
dative case	sim	sinere	sim	siine
common case	unsere	unseri	unser	unseri
dative case	unserem	unserer	unserem	unsere
common case	öire	öiri	öier	öiri
dative case	öirem	öirer	öirem	öirne
common case	iire	iiri	iir	iiri
dative case	iirem	iirer	iirem	iirne

Sali zämme - your Baseldütsch survival guide

Verbs

Survival verbs

	inf.	ich	du	är	miir	diir	sii
be	sii	bi	bisch	isch	sinn	sind	sinn
become	wäärde	wird	wirsch	wird	wäärde	wäärdet	wäärde
come	koo	kumm	kunnsch	kunnt	kömme	kömmet	kömme
do	due	due	duesch	duet	dien	diend	dien
drink	dringge	dringg	dringgsch	dringgt	dringge	dringget	dringge
drive	faare	faar	faarsch	faart	faare	faaret	faare
eat	ässe	iss	issisch	isst	ässe	ässet	ässe
give	gää	gib	gisch	git	gänn	gännd	gänn
go	goo	gang	goosch	goot	göön	göönd	göön
have	haa	haa	hesch	hett	hänn	händ	hänn
hear	loose	loos	loosisch	loost	loose	looset	loose
hold	heebe	heb	hebsch	hebt	heebe	heebet	heebe
like	gäärn haa	haa gäärn	hesch gäärn	het gäärn	hänn gäärn	händ gäärn	hänn gäärn
love	liebe	lieb	liebsch	liebt	liebe	liebet	liebe
say	saage	saag	säisch	säit	saage	saaget	saage
see	luege	lueg	luegsch	luegt	luege	lueget	luege
sleep	schloofe	schloof	schloofsch	schlooft	schloofe	schloofet	schloofe
travel	räise	räis	räisisch	räist	räise	räiset	räise
walk	lauffe	lauff	lauffsch	laufft	lauffe	lauffet	lauffe
want	möcht	möcht	möchtsch	möcht	möchte	möchtet	möchte
wash	wäsche	wäsch	wäschisch	wäscht	wäsche	wäschet	wäsche
work	schaffe	schaff	schaffsch	schafft	schaffe	schaffet	schaffe

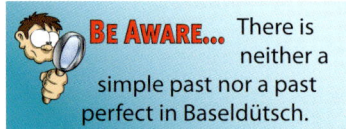 **Be Aware...** There is neither a simple past nor a past perfect in Baseldütsch.

Appendix

Other common past tenses (perfect tense)

Ich bi gsii	I have been / I was
Ich haa gmacht	I have made / I made
Ich haa drungge	I have drunk / I drank
Ich haa gässe	I have eaten / I ate
Ich haa gschloofe	I have slept / I slept
Ich bi gloffe	I have walked / I walked
Ich bi gange	I have gone / I went
Ich haa gloost	I have listened / I listened
Ich haa gschafft	I have worked / I worked
Ich bi gfaare	I have driven / I drove
I ha gluegt	I have watched / I watched

TIP... The past in German is built with the verb **haa** (have) + the past participle:
Ich haa d Uffzgi gmacht (I did my homework).

Some verbs (usually movements) build the past with the verb **sii** (to be) + the past participle:
Ich bii uf Züüri gange (I went to Zurich).

Modal verbs

	Infin.	1 sing.pres	2 sing.pres.	1+3 pl.pres.
can	könne	kaa	kasch	könne
like	mööge	maag	maagsch	mööge
may	döörfe	daarf	döörfsch / daarfsch	döörfe
must	miesse	muess	muesch	mien
should	sölle	soll / söll	söllsch	solle / sölle
want	welle	wott / will	wotsch	wänn

Dictionary

Dictionary

English – Baseldütsch
Baseldütsch – English

Sali zämme - your Baseldütsch survival guide

English-Baseldütsch

A

a pair	e baar (weenigi) veräinzelti
abdomen	Buuch (m)
above	über
abscess	Abszäss (m)
across	über
across from	geegenüüber wisawii
address	Adrässe (f)
address book	Adrässbuech (n)
adult	Erwaggsene (m) Erwaggseni (f)
advertising	Wäärbig (f)
aeroplane	Fluugzüüg (n)
afraid	ängschtlig
after	noch
afternoon	Nomidaag (m)
against	geege
airmail	Luftboscht (f)
allergic to ...	alergisch uff ...
allergy	Aleergii (f)
along	entlang
altimeter	Hööemässer (m)
amazed	erstuunt
ambulance	Ambulanz (f) Granggenauti (f) Saniteet (f)
angry	böös
ankle	Gnöchel (m)
anniversary	Jubilääum
answering machine	Delifonbeantworter (m)
ant	Aamäise (f)
antidote	Geegemittel (n)
anxious	ängschtlig
anything	irgendöppis
appendicitis	Blinddarmenzündig (f)
appetizer	Aperitif (m)
apple	Öpfel (m)
appointment	Termiin (m)
appraisal	Läischtigsbewäärtig (f) Qualifikazioon (f)
apprentice	Leerling (m)
April	April (m)
area code	Vorwaal (f)
argue (verb)	händle / kääre stritte
argument	Buff (n)
argument	Händel (m) / Striit (m) Lämpe (plur.)
arm	Aarm (m)
around	um
arrival	Aakunft (f)
art	Kunscht (f)
article	Ardiggel (m)
Aspirin	Aschpiriin (n)
assistant	Assischtänt (m) Assischtäntin (f)
asthma	Aschtma (n)
at	bi
at /on (vert. surface)	am / an
attachment	aaghängti Datei (f) Aahang (m) / Aalaag (f) Biilaag (f)
attic	Eschtrig (m)
attic flat	Attikawoonig (f) Dachwoonig (f)
August	Auguscht (m)
aunt	Dante (f)
autumn	Herbscht (m)
avalanche	Lawiine

B

B&B	B&B (n)
baby	Buscheli (n) Buschi(n)
baby bottle	Schobbe (m)
baby boy	Biebli (n)
baby food	Breili (n)
baby girl	Mäiteli (n)
baby sling	Draagduech (n)
baccalaureate degree	Maduur (f)
baccalaureate school	Gimmeli (n) Gimnaasium (n)
back	Rugge (m)
backpack	Schuelsagg (m) Ruggsagg (m)
bacon	Spägg (m)
bad	schlächt
bad luck	Bäch
bag	Däsche (f)
baguette	Pariiserbroot (n)
bakery	Begg (m) Beggerei (f)
balcony	Balkon (m)
banana	Banaane (f)
bandage	Verband (m)
Band-aid	Pfläschterli (n)
bank	Bangg (f)
bank account	Banggkonto (n)
banknote	Banggnoote (f)
bar	Baar (f)
barbecue	Grillfescht (n)
basement	Käller (m)
basement garage	Diefgaraasch (f)
bath tub	Baadwanne (f)
bathroom	Baadzimmer (n)
be careful	Achtung
beach	Strand (m)
beans	Boone (f)
bear	Bäär (m)

Dictionary

beautiful	schöön
become (verb)	wäärde
bed	Bett (n)
bed cover	Bettaazug (m)
bedroom	Schloofzimmer (n)
bedtime story	Guetnacht-Gschichtli (n)
bee	Biene (f) / Bienli (n)
beef	Rindfläisch (n)
beer	Bier (n)
beetle	Kääfer (m)
behind	hinder
beige	beesch
bellybutton	Buuchnaabel (m)
belt	Gürtel (m) / Guurt (m)
beneath	under
beside	nääbe
betrayed	bedrooge
between	zwüsche
bib	Ässmänteli (n)
bicycle	Welo (n)
big	gross
Bird	Voogel (m)
biro	Kulli (m)
birthday	Gebuurtsdaag
birthday party	Gebuurtsdaags-Paarti
bitter	bitter
black	schwaarz
blink (verb)	blinzle
blood	Bluet (n)
blood pressure	Bluetdrugg (m)
blood sugar	Bluetzugger (m)
blouse	Bluuse (f)
blow one's nose	sich d Naase butze
blue	blau
blush (verb)	root wärde
board (verb)	boorde / snööbe
board of directors	Verwaltigsroot (m)
body lotion	Köörpermilch (f)
boiled	kocht
bonus	Boonus (m)
book	Buech (n)
book shelves	Biechergstell (n)
bookshop	Biecherlaade (m) / Buechhandlig (f)
bored	glangwiilt
boss	Scheff (m) *(franz.: chef)* / Scheffin (f)
bottom	Fuudi (n)
bowl	Schüssle (f)
box	Kischte (f) / Schachtle (f)
boy	Bueb (m)
boyfriend	Fründ (m)
bra	Beehaa (BH) (m)
brand	Maargge (f)
bread	Broot (n)
break	Pause (f)
breakfast	Zmoorge (m)
breast	Bruscht (f) / Buuse (f)
bridge	Brugg (f)
briefcase	Aarbetsmappe (f) / Mappe (f)
broccoli	Broggoli (m)
broken bone	Gnochebruch (m)
brother	Brueder (m)
brother-in-law	Schwooger (m)
brown	bruun
brown bread	dunggels Broot (n)
brunch	Bröntsch (m)
brush	Bürschte (f)
bug	Wäntele (f)
building	Geböid (n)
bull	Stier (m)
bulletin board	Aaschlagbrätt (n) / schwarzes Brätt (n)
bunker	Bunker (m) / Luftschutzkäller (m)
burn (verb)	brenne
burned	verbrennt
burp	goorbse
burp (baby)	göörbsle
bus	Bus (m)
bus station	Busbaanhoof (m)
bus stop	Bushaltstell (f)
bus ticket	Busbilljee (n)
business casual	unzwunge
butcher's shop	Metzgerei (f)
butter	Angge (m)
button	Gnopf (m)
buy (verb)	boschte / bsoorge / kauffe
buzzard	Möisebussard (m)
by	bim / bi
Bye	Tschau / Tschüss / Adiöö (franz.: adieu) / Uff Wiidersee / Uff Wiiderluege

C

cable TV	Kaabelfäärnsee (n)
cafe	Kaffi (n)
cake	Doorte (f) / Kueche (m)
call (verb)	aalütte / e Fungg gää
camping	Kämping (n)
can (verb)	könne
cancel (verb)	lösche
candy	Dääfeli (n) / Dääfi (n)
canteen	Kantiine (f) / Mensa (f)
cap	Kappe (f) / Tschäpper (m)
cappuccino	Gabbudschiino (m) / Gabbuudscho (m) *(ital.: Cappuccino)*
car	Auto (n)
care of	zuhande vo
Carnival	Faasnacht (f)
carpet	Deppig (m)
carrots	Riebli (n)
cash	Baar (n) / Baargäld (n)
cash machine	Banggomaat (m) / Boschtomaat (m) / Gäldautomat (m)
cashier	Kassierer (m) / Kassierere (f)
cat	Buusi (n) / Buusle (f) / Kaater (m) / Katz (f) / Maudi (m)
Cathedral	Kathedraale (f) / Münschter (n)
cauliflower	Bluemekool (m)
celebrity	Promi (m) / Vip (m) (VIP)
cellar	Käller (m)
cell phone	Händi (n) / Natel (n)
century	Joorhundert (n)
chair	Stuel (m)
chair lift	Sässelilift (m)
chamois	Gäms (f) / Gämsi (n)
champagne (glass)	Güppli (n)
changing table	Wiggeldisch (n)
channel	Kanaal (m)
cheat (verb)	abluege / bschisse / spigge
check in	ii-tschegge
check out	uss-tschegge
cheek	Bagge (m)
cheerful	fröölig / häiter / uffgstellt
cheers	Santee / Broscht
cheese	Kääs (m)
cheque	Schegg (m)
cherry	Kiirsi (n)
chest	Bruscht (f) / Buuse (m)
chicken	Güggeli (n) / Huen (n)
children	Kinder
children's room	Kinderzimmer (n)
chimney	Kemmi (n)
Christmas	Wienacht
church	Kirche (f)
cider	suure Moscht (m)
cigarette	Zigerette
cinema	Kiino (n)
city	Innerstadt (f) / Stadt (f)
city map	Stadtblaan (n)
cleaner	Butzfrau (f) / Butzmaa (m)
clear	häll
climate	Kliima (n)
clinic	Kliinik (f)
close (verb)	schliesse / zuedue / zuemache
closed	zue (adj.)
closet	Kaschte (m)
clothing	Gläider (pl)
cloudy	bedeggt /bewölkt
coat	Mantel (m)
cockroach	Schwoobekääfer (m)
code	Ghäimnummerä (f) / Kood (m) / Pinnkood (m)
coffee (w/cream)	Kaffi Greem (m) *(franz.: Café crème)*
coffee bar	Kaffi (n)

Sali zämme - your Baseldütsch survival guide

English	Baseldütsch
coffee break	Kaffipause (f)
coffee party	Kaffiklatsch (m)
	Kaffikränzli (n)
coffee with milk	Milchkaffi (m)
	Schaale (f)
coin	Münze (f)
cold	kalt
cold	Verkeltig (f)
collar	Graage (m)
colleague	Aarbetskolleeg (m)
	Aarbetskolleegin (f)
collect (verb)	sammle
comb	Strääl (m)
come (verb)	koo
commission	Komissioon (f)
complain	joomere / mozze
	reklamiere
	sich beklaage
	wäffele
concert	Konzäärt (n)
concierge	Gonsiersch
	(franz.: concierge)
concussion	Hiirnerschütterig (f)
condiment	Gwüürz (pl)
condom	Gummi (m)
	Kondoom (n)
	Pariiser (m)
conference	Komferänz (f)
congratulations	Gratulazioon
connection	Verbindig (f)
consultant	Berooter (f/m)
contagious	aasteggend
continent	Kontinänt (m)
contraceptive	Verhietigsmittel (n)
contract	Verdraag (m)
cool (feeling)	kuul
cool (temperature)	früsch / kiel
copy	kopiere
corn	Mäis (m)
corn on the cob	Mäiskolbe (m)
corner	Egge (m)
costs	Koschte (pl)
cosy	gmietlig
cot	Kinderbett (n)
cotton	Bauele (f)
	Baumwulle (f)
cough (verb)	hueschte
counter	Schalter (m)
country	Land (n)
county	Kantoon (m)
course	Kuurs (m)
cousin	Guusäng (m)
	Guusiine (f)
cover	zueheebe
cow	Kue (f)
crab	Krabbe (f)
cramp	Grampf (m)
crazy	gspunne / irr
	verruggt
cream	Greeme (f) / Raam (m)
credit card	Kreditkaarte (f)
crib	Kinderbett (n)
crocodile	Groggedill (n)

English	Baseldütsch
croissant	Gipfeli (n)
cross country skiing	langlauffe
crossing	Abzwiigig (f)
	Grüzzig (f)
cry	briele / griine / hüüle
culture	Kultuur (f)
cup	Dasse (f)
curd cheese	Quaark (m)
currency	Väärig (f)
curtains	Voorhäng (pl)
customer	Kund (m)
	Kundin (f)
customs	Zoll (m)
cutlery	Bstegg (n)

D

English	Baseldütsch
dance	danze
dark	dunkel
daughter	Dochter (f)
daughter-in-law	Schwiigerdochter (f)
dawn	Dämmerig (f)
	Moorgedämmerig (f)
day	Daag (m)
daycare	Krippe (f)
debit card	Boschtkaarte (f)
	Eezee-Kaarde (f)
	(EC-Kaarde)
decade	zää Joor (f)
December	Dezämber (m)
declare (at customs)	verzolle
deep fried	frittieert
deer	Hirsch (m)
delay	Verspöötig (f)
deli (catessen)	Delikatesselaade (m)
delicious	fein / heerlig
deodorant	Deo (m)
department	Abdäilig (f)
Department store	Waarehuus (n)
departure	Abräis (f)
deposit	Deppo (n)
	Hinderleegig (f)
depressed	depressiiv
desk	Pult (n)
desktop	Aarbetsflechi (m)
	Schriibtisch (m)
desperate	verzwiiflet
dessert	Dessert (m)
detergent	Wöschmittel (n)
diabetes	Diabeetes (f)
	Zugger (m)
diabetic	diabeetisch
diapers	Windle (pl)
diarrhoea	Durchfall (m)
diet	Diäät (f)
digestive	Didchestiif (m)
	(franz.: digestive)
digestive	Vertäilerli (m)
dining car	Spiiswaage (m)
dining room	Ässzimmer (n)
dinner	Znacht (m)
	Znachtässe (n)
dinner service	Gschirr (n) / Service (n)

English	Baseldütsch
direction sign	Wägwiiser (m)
director	Diräggder (m)
	Diräggdere (f)
	Diräggdoorin (f)
disappointed	enttüscht
discotheque	Disco (f)
discount	aabegesetzt
	reduziert
discount	Verbilligung (f)
dishes	Gschiir (n)
dishwasher	Abwäschmaschiine (f)
divorced	gschiide
doctor	Aarzt (m)
	Doggder (m)
	Äärztin (f)
	Doggdere (f)
doctor's surgery	Praxis (f)
dog	Hund (m)
donkey	Eesel (m)
door	Düür (f)
doorbell	Huusglogge (f)
double bed	Doppelbett (n)
down	aabe
download (verb)	aabelaade
draft beer	Stange (f)
drawer	Schuublaade (f)
dress	Aazuug (m) / Gläid (n)
dress (verb)	aaleege
dress code	Gläiderknigge (f)
	Gläidervoorschrift (f)
dressed	aaglegt
dressing	Salaatsoosse (f)
drill (verb)	oggse
drill (verb)	büffle
	schanze
drink (verb)	dringge
drive (fast)	raase
driving licence	Billjee (n)
	Faaruuswiis (m)
drops	Dröpfli (pl)
drugs	Drooge (pl)
dry	drogge
dry out	uusdroggne
dummy	Nuggi (m)
dusk	Dämmerig (f)
	Oobedämmerig (f)
duvet	Deggi (f)

E

English	Baseldütsch
eagle	Aadler (m)
ear	Oor (n)
early	frie
earn money	Gäld verdiene
easy hill to ski	Idiottehüügel (m)
eat (verb)	ässe
editor	Herusgääber (m)
	Herusgääbere (f)
egg	Äi (n)
eggplant	Oberschiine (f)
eight	acht
eighteen	achzää
eighty	achzig

Dictionary

English	Dialect
elbow	Ell(e)booge (m)
electrical shop	Elektrogschäft (n)
elementary	Brimaarschuel (f)
	Brimmeli (f)
elephant	Elefant (m)
eleven	elf
e-mail	Ii-Meil (n) / Meil (n)
emergency	Nootfall (m)
emergency exit	Nootussgang (m)
emergency room	Nootuffnaam (f)
emigrate (verb)	ussräise
employee	Aagstellte (m)
	Aagstellti (f)
employer	Aarbetgääber (m)
	Aarbetgääbere (f)
engaged	bsetzt / verlobt
English	Änglisch
entertainment	Underhaltig (f)
entrance	Iigang (m)
envelope	Guweer (n)
	(franz.: Couvert)
envious	iifersüchtig
	niidisch
equipment	Ussrüschtig (f)
eraser	Gummi (m)
espresso	Espresso (m)
estate agency	Verwaltig (f)
European ibex	Stäibogg (m)
even numbers	graadi Zaale
evening	Oobe (m)
evening dress	Oobegläid (n)
event	Aaloss (m)
exam	Briefig (f)
exchange rate	Wäggselkuurs (f)
excited	uffgreggt
excuse me	Entschuldigung
	Exgüüsi (franz.: excusez)
exhibition	Uss-stellig (f)
exit	Ussgang (m)
expensive	düür
eye	Aug (n)
eyebrow	Augebraue (f)
eyelash	Wimpere (pl)

F

face	Gsicht (n)
fall down (verb)	umfalle / umfliege
	umgheie
family	Familie
family get together	Familieschluuch (m)
	Familiezämmekunft (f)
famous	beriemt / bekannt
fantastic	fantastisch
farewell party	Abschiidsfescht (n)
fashion	Moode (f)
father	Vatter (m)
father-in-law	Schwiigervatter (m)
faucet	Haane (m)
February	Februaar (m)
fee	Briis (m) / Gebüür (f)
fever	Fieber (n)
few	weenig

English	Dialect
fiancé	Verlobte (m)
fiancée	Verlobti (f)
field	Fäld (n)
fifteen	fuffzää
fifty	fuffzig
fine	guet / fein
finger	Finger (m)
fingernail	Fingernaagel (m)
fire	Füür
fire department	Füürweer (f)
first	erscht
first aid	Erschti Hiilf (f)
first floor	der erschti Stock
fish	Fisch (m)
fish (verb)	fische
fitness	Fitness
five	fümf
flag	Faane (f)
flavour	Gschmagg (m)
floor	Boode (m)
flour	Määl (n)
flu	Grippe (f)
fly	Fliege (f)
fog	Nääbel (m)
fold	falte
foot	Fuess (m)
footpath	Wääg (m)
for	für
forecast	Wätterbricht (m)
forehead	Stiirne (f)
foreigner	Ussländer (m)
	Ussländere (f)
forest	Wald (m)
fork	Gaable (f)
form	Formulaar (n)
forty	vierzig
forward	witerläite
fountain pen	Fülli (n)
four	vier
fourteen	vierzää
fox	Fuggs (m)
freckles	Laubflägge (pl)
	Summersprosse (pl)
freelance	äigeständig
freezer	Diefkieler (m)
fresh	früsch
Friday	Fritig
fridge	Iiskaschte (m)
fried	brääglet
friend	Fründ (m) / Fründin (f)
from	us / vo
from where?	Vo woo?
frontier / border	Gränze (f)
frozen	diefgfroore
fruit	Frucht (f)
frying pan	Brootpfanne (f)
full board	Vollbangsioon (f)
full time	Vollziit
funny	luschtig / witzig
furious	hässig
future	Zuekumft (f)
	zuekümftig
	in Zuekumft

G

gamble (verb)	spiile
game	Spiil (n)
garage	Garaasch (f)
	(franz.: garage)
	Iistellhalle (f)
garden	Gaarte (m)
garlic	Knooblauch (m)
gay	schwuul
geography	Geografii (f)
girl	Mäitli (n)
girlfriend	Fründin (f)
give (verb)	gää
glass	Glaas (n)
glasses	Brülle (pl)
gloves	Händsche (pl)
go (verb)	goo
goat	Gäiss (f)
gold	goldig
good	guet
good afternoon	Guete Nomidaag
good evening	Gueten Oobe
good morning	Guete Moorge
goose bumps	Hienerhutt (f)
gossip	Grätsch (n)
	Klatsch (m)
	Tratsch (m)
gossip (verb)	klatsche / rätsche
	traatsche
grab (verb)	griiffe / länge
grandchild	Grosskind (n)
granddaughter	Änkelin (f)
	Grossdochter (f)
grandfather	Grossvatter (m)
grandmother	Grossmueter (f)
grandparents	Grosseltere (pl)
grandson	Änkel (m)
	Grosssoon (m)
grateful	danggbaar
great aunt	Grossdante (f)
great grandfather	Uurgrossvatter (m)
great grandmother	Uurgrossmueter (f)
great uncle	Grossunggle (m)
green	grien
grey	grau
grill	Grill (m)
grill area	Füürstell (f)
grilled	grilieert
groceries	Lääbesmittel (pl)
ground floor	Baarteer (n)
	(franz.: parterre)
guinea pig	Meersöili (n)
gutter	Dachkäänel (n)
gym	Fitnessruum (m)
gymnasium (school)	Gimmeli (n)
	Gimnaasium (n)

H

English	Dialect
hail	Haagel (m)
hail (verb)	haagle
hair	Hoor (pl)

141

Sali zämme - your Baseldütsch survival guide

English	Baseldütsch
half board	Halbbangsioon (f)
hallway	Gang (m)
ham	Schingge (m)
hand	Hand (f)
hand cream	Handgreeme (f)
hand dryer	Händedroggner (m)
hanger	Gläiderbüügel (m)
happy	glügglig
hat	Huet (m)
have (verb)	haa
hay fever	Höischnuppe (m)
he	är
head	Kopf (m)
headache	Kopfwee (n)
headlines	Schlaagziile (pl)
health	Gsundhäit
health insurance	Granggekasse (f)
hear	hööre
heart	Häärz (n)
heat	Hitz (f)
hello	Griezi
help	Hiilfe (f)
hen night	Bolteroobe (m)
here	doo
heterosexual	hetero(sexuell)
hi	Sali / Salli
high school	Sekundaarschuel (f)
highway/motorway	Autobaan (f)
hiking	wandere
hiking path	Wanderwääg (m)
hiking shoes	Wanderschue (pl)
hill	Hüügel (m)
hip	Huft / Hüfte (f)
hippopotamus	Niilpfäärd (n)
hold (verb)	heebe
home	häi
home owner	Huusbsitzer /e (m/f)
homework	Huus-Uffgoobe (f)
homework	Uffgoobe (pl)
homosexual	homo(sexuell)
honey	Hoonig (m)
horny	giggerig / spitz
horse	Ross (n)
hospital	Spidaal (n)
hot	häiss
hot chocolate	Häissi Schoggi (f)
hot milk	Häissi Milch (f)
hot wine	Glüewii (m)
hour	Stund (f)
house	Huus (n)
house number	Huusnummere (f)
housewarming party	Huusiiweiigs-Paarti (f)
how long?	Wie lang?
how many?	Wie viil?
how much?	Wie viil?
how?	Wie?
hug	umaarme
humid	fiecht
humour	Humoor (m)
hundred thousand	hundertdausig / hundertduusig
hurry	schnäll
husband	Maa (m)

I

English	Baseldütsch
I	ich
ice	lis
ice cream	Glasse (n) (franz.: glace)
immigrate (verb)	iiräise
in / into	in
in a moment	glii
in a moment	graad
in front of	voor
in love	verliebt
income	likomme (n)
infection	Enzündig (f)
injection	Sprützi (f)
injury	Verletzig (f)
insect	Inseggt (n)
insomnia	Schloofloosikäit (f)
insurance	Versicherig (f)
insurance number	Versicherigs-Nummere (f)
intensive care	Intensiivstazioon (f)
interest	Zins (m)
international news	Ussland-Noochrichte (pl)
internet connection	Internetaaschluss
into	geege
invest money	Gäld inweschtiere
investment	Inweschtizioon (f)
invoice	Rächnig (f)
iron	Glettiise (n)
iron (verb)	glette
island	Insle (f)

J

English	Baseldütsch
jack salmon	Zander (m)
jackdaw	Doole (f)
jacket	Jagge (f)
jam	Gomfi (f)
jam doughnut	Berliiner (m)
jam jar	Gomfiglaas (n)
January	Januaar (m)
jealous	iifersüchtig
jeans	Tschiins (pl)
job application	Bewäärbig (f)
job description	Pflichteheft (n)
job interview	Bewäärbigsgsprööch (n)
joke	Witz (m)
joyful	froo / zfriide
July	Juli (m)
jump (verb)	gumpe / springe
June	Juni (m)

K

English	Baseldütsch
key	Schlüssel (m)
kilo	Kilo (n)
kindergarten	Hääfelischuel (m) / Kindergaarte (m) / Kindsgi (m)
kiss	Kuss
kiss (verb)	schmuuse
kitchen	Kuchi (f)
kitchen cupboard	Kuchikäschtli (n)
knee	Gnöi (n)
knife	Mässer (n)
kosher	kooscher

L

English	Baseldütsch
laboratory	Laboor (n)
lake	See (m)
lamb	Lamm (n)
land	lande
landlord	Vermieter (m) / Vermietere (f)
laptop	Läppi (m) / Läptop (m)
large	gross
late	spoot
latte macchiato	Latte Maggiaaddo (n) (ital.: latte macchiato)
laugh	lache
laundry	Wösch (f)
laundry bag	Wöschsagg (m)
laundry basket	Wöschkorb (m) / Wöschzäine (f)
laundry day	Wöschdaag (m)
laundry room	Wöschkuchi (f)
laundry schedule	Wöschblaan (m)
lawn	Raase (m)
lawnmower	Raasemäier (m)
learn (verb)	leere
leather	Lääder (n)
leave	abfaare
left	linggs
leg	Bäi (n)
legumes	Hülsefrücht (pl)
lemon	Zitroone (f)
lentils	Linse (pl)
lesbian	lesbisch
less	weeniger
letter	Brief (m)
lettuce	Kopfsalaat (m)
library	Bibliotheek (f)
lick	lutsche
life	Lääbe (n)
lift	Lift (m)
lightning	Blitz (m)
like (verb)	gäärn haa / mööge
lilac	lila
lime	Limoone (f)
linen	Liine (f)
lion	Löi (m)
listen (verb)	loose
litre	Liter (m)
liver	Lääbere (f)
lizard	Äideggsli (n)
loan	Darleehe (n)
lobby	Hotelhalle (f) / ligangshalle (f) / Voorruum (m)
lobster	Hummer (m)

Dictionary

local news	lokaali Nöiigkäite (pl)	mild	mild	**O**	
	Lokaal-Noochrichte (pl)	milk	Milch (f)		
log in	aamälde / iilogge	millennium	Joordausig (n)	obituary	Doodesaazäig (f)
log out	abmälde / usslogge		Joorduusig (n)	occupation	Bruef (m) / Tschob (m)
lonely	äinsaam	minus	minus	ocean	Ozeaan (n)
long	lang	minute	Minute (f)	October	Oggtoober (m)
long sleeves	langeermlig	minutes	Brotokoll (n)	odd numbers	ungraadi Zaale
look (verb)	luege	mirror	Spiegel (m)	of	vo
loss	Verluscht (m)	mobile phone	Händi (n) / Natel (n)	office	Büüro (n) / Gschäft (n)
lounge	Stuube (f)	moment	Momänt (m)	old building	Altbau (m)
love (verb)	gäärn haa / liebe	Monday	Määntig	old man	alte Maa (m)
lovely	häärzig	money	Gäld (n)	old woman	alti Frau (f)
lucky number	Glüggszaal (f)	monkey	Aff (m)	olive oil	Oliivenööl (n)
luggage	Gepäck (n)	month	Moonet (m)	on (horiz. surface)	uff
lunch	Zmittag (m)	more	mee	on foot	z Fuess
	Zmittagässe (n)	morning	Moorge (m)	on sale	Ussverkauf
lunch break	Mittagspause (f)	mosque	Moschee (f)	on time	pünggtlig
lynx	Luggs (m)	mosquito	Mugge (f)	one	äins
		mother	Mueter (f)	one billion	e Milliarde (f)
M		mother-in-law	Schwiigermueter (f)	one hundred	hundert
		mountain	Bäärg (m)	one million	e Million (f)
magazine	Heftli (n)	mouse	Muus (f) / Müüsli (n)	one thousand	dausig / duusig
magic	Zauberei (f)	mouth	Muul (n)	one-room flat	Äizimmerwoonig (n)
magic (verb)	zaubere (Verb)	move out (v)	uuszie	onion	Ziibele (f)
mailbox	Briefkaschte (m)	much	viil	open (adj.)	offe
main course	Hauptspiis (f)	museum	Museeum (n)	open (verb)	uffmache
make-up	Schminkzüüg (n)	music	Muusig (f)	opera	Oopere (f)
manager	Mänätscher (m)	must (verb)	miesse	operation	Operazioon (f)
	Mänätschere (f)			opinion	Mäinig (f)
many	viil	**N**		opposite	geegenüüber
map	Kaarte (f)				wisawii
	Stadtblaan (f)	nail	Naagel (m)	orange	Orangsche (f)
march	Meerz (m)	name	Naame	orange (colour)	orangsch
margarine	Maargeriine (f)	napkin	Serviette (f)	order (verb)	bstelle
marinated	marinieert	nappies	Windle (pl)	oven	Baggoofe (m)
marital status	Ziviilstand (m)	national news	Inland-Noochrichte (pl)	over	über
marmalade	Orangschegomfi (f)	neck	Ägge (m)	over salted	versalze
marmot	Mungg (m)	neighbours	Noochbere (pl)	overtime	Üüberstunde (pl)
	Muurmeldier (n)	nephew	Neffe (m) / Nöwöö (m)	owner	Bsitzer (m) /Bsitzere (f)
	Muurmeli (n)	new building	Nöibau (m)		
marriage	Ee (f)	news	Noochrichte (pl)	**P**	
married	ghüüroote	newspaper	Daageszitig (f)		
marten	Maarder (m)		Zitig (f)	pacifier	Nuggi (m)
mash	Breili (n)	next to	nääbe	packet	Päckli (n)
massage	Massaasch (f)	niece	Nichte (f)	pain	Schmäärze (pl) / Wee
	(franz.: massage)	night	Nacht (f)	pain killer	Schmäärzmittel (n)
maturity diploma	Maduur (f)	nine	nüün	painful	schmäärzhaft
May	Mäi (m)	nineteen	nüünzää	pan	Pfanne (f)
may (verb)	döörfe	ninety	nüünzig	panties	Underhoose (f)
meals	Moolzite (pl)	nipple	Bruschtwaarze (f)	paper towel	Bapiirhandtuech (n)
meat	Fläisch (n)	no	Näi	paragliding	Gläitschirm fliege
medicine	Medikamänt	no smoking	Nichtraucher	parasite	Parasit (m)
	Häilmittel (n)	noon	Mittag (m)	park	Paark (m)
medium (meat)	meedium / halbduure	nose	Naase (f)	parking area	Paarkblatz (m)
medium (size)	mittel / mittelgross	nothing	nüt	part time	Däilzit
meeting	Besprächig (f)	november	Novämber (m)	partner	Lääbespaartner (m)
	Sitzig (f)	now	Geegewaart (f)		Lääbespaartnere (f)
men	Männer		im Momänt / jetz		Paartner (m)
men's toilet	Herredualette (pl)		momäntaan / zer Zit		Paartnere (f)
	Männerweezee	nurse	Granggepflääger (m)	party	Fescht (n)
menu	Spiiskarte		Granggeschwescher (f)		Paarti (f)
microwave	Mikrowälle (f)	nurse (verb)	stille		
midday	Mittag (m)	nylon	Näilen (n)		

143

Sali zämme - your Baseldütsch survival guide

English	Baseldütsch
passenger	Faargascht, Passaschier (m)
passport	Bass (m)
past	umme / verbii vergange
past	Vergangehäit (f)
pasta	Däigwaare (pl)
pastry	Gebäck (n), Stüggli (pl)
path	Wääg (m)
patient	Baziert (m), Baziäntin (f)
pay (verb)	zaale
payment	Zaalig (f)
peak	Gipfel (m)
peanut butter	Äärdnussangge (m)
pear	Biire (f)
pediatrician	Kinderaarzt (m), Kinderäärztin (f)
pen	Kulli (m)
pencil	Bleistift (m)
penis	Peenis (m) / Pfiffli (n)
pension fund	Bangsioonskasse (f)
pepper	Peperooni (f)
perch	Eegli (m)
permit	Bewilligung (f), Genäämigung (f)
petrol	Benziin (n), Moscht (m)
petrol station	Tankstell (f)
phone call	Aaruef (m) / Delifon (n), Fungg (m)
phone number	Delifonnummere (f)
photo	Fotteli (n) / Fotti (f)
picnic	Piggnigg (n)
pie	Wääie (f)
pig	Sau (f)
pike	Hächt (m)
pill	Dablette (f) / Pille (f)
pillow	Küssi (n)
pink	roosa
plan	Blaan (m)
plane ticket	Fluugbilljee (n)
plate	Däller (m)
platform	Perron (n)
play (verb)	spiile
play football	schutte
please	Bitte
plug	Stegger (m)
plus	und / plus
poison	Gift (n)
poisoned	vergiftet
police	Bolizei (f)
police station	Bolizeiboschte (m)
polyester	Polijeschter (m)
pork	Saufläisch (n), Schwiinigs (n)
post	Boscht (m)
post office	Boscht (f)
postage stamp	Boschtstämpel (m)
postal money order	Gäldüüberwiisig (f)
postcard	Boschtkaarte (f)
postal code	Boschtläitzaal (f)
postman	Böschtler (m), Böschtlere (f), Briefdrääger (m), Briefdräägere (f)
potatoes	Häärdöpfel (m)
pound	Pfund (n)
pram	Kinderwaage (m)
prawns	Riisegrövette (f)
pray	bätte
pregnant	schwanger
prescription	Rezäpt (n)
present	Geegewaart (f), im Momänt / jetz momäntaan / zer Zit
presentation	Presentazioon (f)
press	drugge
pretty	hübsch
price	Briis (m)
primary school	Brimaarschuel (f), Brimmeli (f)
print	drugge
printer	Drugger (m)
professional	Profi (m/f)
profit	Profitt (m)
provisions	Proviant (m)
public telephone	Delifonkabiine (f)
punch	Punnsch (m)
purchase order	Bstellig (f), Uffdraag (m)
purse	Handdäschli (n)

Q

| quiet | rueig |
| quiet area | rueigi Laag (f) |

R

rabbit	Küngel (m)
rabies	Dollwuet (f)
radio	Raadio (m)
rain	Rääge (m)
rain (verb)	räägne
rare (food)	bluetig
raspberry	Himbeeri (n)
raw	roo
razor blades	Rasierklinge (f)
read (verb)	lääse
reception	Empfang (m), Ressepsion (f) (franz.: réception)
receptionist	Ressepzionischt (m), Ressepzionischtin (f)
recess	Pause (f)
red	root
red wine	Roote (m) / Rootwii (m)
registered letter	iigschriibene Brief (m)
registered mail	iigschriibeni Boscht (f)
relatives	Verwandti (pl)
remote control	Fäärnbedienig (f)
rental flat	Mietwoonig (f)
repeat	wiiderhoole
reply	antworte, zruggschriibe
report	Bricht (m)
report card	Züügnis (n)
reserve (verb)	reserviere
residence permit	Uffenthaltsgenäämigung (f)
restaurant	Bäiz (f) / Wiirtschaft (n)
rhinoceros	Naashorn (n)
rice	Riis (m)
right	rächts
river	Fluss (m)
roasted	grööschtet
roe deer	Ree (n)
roll	Bröötli (n) / Büürli (n), Schlumbi (m), Schwööbli (n)
roof	Dach (n)
room	Zimmer (n)
room service	Zimmermäitli (f), Zimmer-Seerwis (m)
rooster	Güggel (m)
rubber	Gummi (m)
rubbish bin	Mischtküübel (m)
rucksack	Ruggsagg (m)

S

sad	druurig
salad	Salaat (m)
salami	Salaami (m)
salary	Loon (m) / Saläär (n)
salesperson	Verköiffer (m), Verköiffere (f)
salmon	Lachs (m)
salty	salzig
sandwich	Sändwidsch (n)
satchel	Schuelsagg (m)
satellite	Satellit (m)
satellite dish	Satelliteschüssle (f)
Saturday	Samschtig
sausage	Wurscht (f)
save (verb)	spaare
savings account	Spaarkonto (n)
say (verb)	saage
scales	Woog (f)
scarf	Fuulaar (m), Schaal (m), Halsduech (n)
school	Schuel (f), Schuelhuus (n)
school bag	Schuelsagg (m)
school report	Züügnis (n)
screen	Bildschiirm (m)
sea	Meer (n)
seafood	Meeresfrücht (pl)
season	Jooreszit (f)
second	Sekunde (f)
secondary school	Sek (f)
secretary	Seggredäär (m), Seggredäärin (f)
section	Abschnitt (m), Däil (m)

Dictionary

security	Sicherhäit (f)
see (verb)	see / luege
self-employed	sälbständig
sell (verb)	verkauffe
send (verb)	schigge
sender's address	Absänder/e (m/f)
sentimental	sentimentaal
separate (verb)	sich drenne
separated	drennt
September	Septämber (m)
service area	Raschtblatz (m)
	Raschtstett (f)
seven	siibe
seventeen	sibzää
seventy	sibzig
sexy	sexi
shake	schüttle
shame	schaad
shampoo	Schampo (n)
sheet	Liinduech (n)
shirt	Hemmli (n)
shoes	Schue (pl)
shop	Laade (m)
shopping (verb)	iikaufe / läädele
shopping bag	Däsche (f)
	Gugge (f)
shopping centre	Iikaufszentrum (n)
short	gläi /kurz
short sleeves	kurzeermlig
shorts	kurzi Hoose (pl)
	Schoorts (pl)
shoulder	Schultere (f)
shower	Duschi (f)
shower cream	Duschmittel (n)
shower curtain	Duschvoorhang (m)
shrimp	Grövette (f)
shy	schüüch
siblings	Gschwischterti (pl)
sick	grangg
signature	Underschrift (f)
silk	Siide (f)
silver	silbrig
single	elläi-steehend
	leedig / singel
sister	Schweschter (f)
sister-in-law	Schwöögere (f)
six	säggs
sixteen	sächzää
sixty	sächzig
ski	Schii (m)
ski boot	Schiischue (m)
ski instructor	Schiileerer (m)
	Schiileerere (f)
ski lift	Schiilift (m)
ski poles	Stögg (pl)
ski school	Schiischuel (m)
skiing	schiifaare
skin	Hutt (f)
skirt	Junte (f) / Rogg (m)
	Schüp (m)
sleep (verb)	schloofe
sleeper	Strampelhoose (m)
sleeping pill	Schloofdablette (f)
sleepy	mied / schlapp
	schlööfrig
slippers	Fingge (pl)
slug	Schnägg (m)
small	gläi
small change	Münz (n) / Münze (pl)
smell	schmegge
smile	lächle
smoking area	Fümuar (n)
	(franz.: fumoir)
	Raucheregge (m)
snack (afternoon)	Zvieri (m)
snack (morning)	Znüüni (m)
snake	Schlange (f)
snow	Schnee (m)
snow shoeing	Schneeschue lauffe
soap	Säiffi (f)
society	Gsellschaft (f)
socks	Sogge (pl)
some	äinigi
somebody	öpper
somehow	irgendwie
something	öppis
sometimes	albe /amme
	männgisch
	männgmool
	öppe / öppedie
somewhere	näime / nöime
son	Soon (m)
son-in-law	Schwiigersoon (m)
soon	bald / glii
sorry	Entschuldigung
	Ojee
	S duet mer läid.
so-so	s goot eso
	so soo la laa
sour	suur
space	Blatz (m) / Ruum (m)
spam	Späm
speak	reede
speed camera	Radaar (m)
speed limit	Gschwindigkäits-
	begränzig (f)
spend (verb)	ussgää / verbutze
	vergänggerle
spicy	schaarf
spider	Spinne (f)
spinach	Spinaat (m)
spirit	Schnaps (m)
spoon	Löffel (m)
sports	Spoort (m)
spring	Frielig (m)
stag night	Bolteroobe (m)
stairs	Stääge (f)
stamp	Briefmaargge (f)
	Maargge (f)
stare	glotze / staarre
starter	Voorspiis (f)
state	Staat (m)
steak	Blätzli (n)
	Schnitzel (n)
	Schteegg (n)
stockings	Strümpf (pl)
stomach	Maage (m)
stomach ache	Buuchwee (n)
store	Laade (m)
storm	Stuurm (m)
stove	Häärd (m)
straight on	graaduss
strawberry	Äärbeeri (n)
street	Strooss (f)
stressed	gstresst
stroller	Kinderwaage (m)
studio	Stuudio (n)
stuffed animal	Blüschdier (n)
stupid	blööd /doof
subject	Bedrääff (m)
successful	erfolgriich
suck	suuge
sugar	Zugger (m)
suit	Aazuug (m)
	Goschdüüm (n)
	Gwändli (n)
	Schaale (f)
summer	Summer (m)
sun	Sunne (f)
Sunday	Sunntig
sunny	sunnig
sunshade	Stoore (m)
	Sunnedach (n)
supermarket	Iikaufszentrum (n)
	Supermäärt (m)
supper	Znacht (n)
suppositories	Zäpfli (n)
surprised	überrascht
sweet	siess
swim (verb)	schwimme
swimming pool	Bassä (n) (franz.: bassin)
	Schwimmbaad (n)
swing	Giigampfi (f) / Ritti (f)
swinging flags	Faaneschwinge
Swiss accordion	Handöörgeli (n)
Swiss army knife	Saggmässer (n)
Swiss franc	Schwizer Frangge (m)
Swiss German	Schwizerdütsch
Swiss trad. music	Ländler (m)
Swiss wrestling	schwinge
symbol '@'	Affeschwanz (m)
	Ät (m)
synagogue	Siinagooge (f)
syrup	Siirup (m)

T

table	Disch (m)
table cloth	Dischduech (n)
table mats	Dischset (n)
take away	Imbiss-Stand (m)
take away (verb)	zum Mitnää
talk show	Gsprööchsrundi (f)
	Talk Show (engl.)
tampon	Tampon (m)
tangerine	Manderiinli (n)
tap	Haane (m)
tasteless	faad / gschmaggloos
taxes	Stüüre (pl)
tea	Tee (m)

Sali zämme - your Baseldütsch survival guide

English	Baseldütsch
teach (verb)	leere
teacher	Leerere (f) /Leerer (m)
teaspoon	Teelöffeli (n)
technician	Techniker (m)
	Technikere (f)
teenager	Tiini (m)
teeth (verb)	zaane
telephone (verb)	aalütte / e Fungg gää
telephone bill	Delifonrächnig (f)
telephone book	Delifonbuech (n)
telephone card	Delifonkaarte(f)
telephone number	Delifonnummere
television	Fäärnsee (n)
television licence	Fäärnseebewilligung (f)
temperature	Temperatuur (f)
ten	zää
tenant	Mieter (m)
	Mietere (f)
tennis Shoes	Dennisschue (pl)
terrace	Terrasse (f)
test	Tescht (m)
text message	SMS (n)
thank you	Dangge
	Meersi *(franz.: merci)*
theatre	Theaater (n)
there	döört
they	sii
thief	Dieb
thing	Ding (n) / Sach (f)
thirteen	drizää
thirty	drissig
three	drei
throat	Hals (m)
through	dur
thunder	Donner (m)
thunderstorm	Gwitter (n)
Thursday	Donnschtig
ticket	Billjee (n)
tie	Grawatte (f)
tiger	Diiger (m)
to where?	Wo aane?
toast	Tooscht (m)
today	hütt(e)
toe	Zeeche (m)
toenail	Zeechenaagel (m)
together	zämme
toilet	Weezee (n)
	Dualette (f)
	(franz.: Toilette)
toilet paper	Dualette-Papiir (n)
	Weezee-Papiir (n)
toiletries	Dualettesache (pl)
toiletry bag	Nessesseer (n)
	(franz.: nécessaire)
tomato	Domaate (f)
tomorrow	moorn
tongue	Zunge (f)
tooth	Zaan (m)
toothache	Zaanwee
toothbrush	Zaanbürschtli (n)
toothpaste	Zaanbaschta (f)
top	Oberdail (n)
top floor	der oberschti Stock
touch (verb)	aalänge / beriere
tourist	Turischt (m)
	Turischtin (f)
towel	Diechli (n)
	Wäschblätz (m)
town	Stadt (f)
track	Gläis (n)
traffic light	Ample (f)
train	Zuug (m)
train station	Baanhoof (m)
train ticket	Zugbilljee (n)
trainee	Praktikant (m)
	Praktikantin (f)
transfer (verb)	überwiise
trash	Abfall (m)
	Bapiirkoorb (m)
travel (verb)	räise
travelers cheques	Schegg (pl)
treasure (little)	Schätzli
tree	Baum (m)
trousers	Hoose (f)
trout	Forälle (f)
T-shirt	Liibli (n)
Tuesday	Zischtig
tumble drier	Tömbler (m)
tuna	Doon (m)
turkey	Druthaan (m)
turtle	Schildgrot (f)
twelve	zwölf
twenty	zwanzig
twins	Zwilling (pl)
two	zwäi
two hundred	zwäihundert
two thousand	zwäidausig
	zwäiduusig
two-level flat	Mesonett-Woonig (f)
	(franz.: Maisonette)
two-room flat	Zwäizimmer-
	Woonig (f)

U

English	Baseldütsch
uncle	Unggle (m)
under	under
underwear	Underwösch (f)
unemployed	aarbetsloos
uniform	Unifoorm (f)
university	Uni (f)
	Universideet (f)
unlucky number	Unglüggszaal (f)
until	bis
up	uffe
urinal	Pissuar (n) *(franz.: Pissoir)*
utility room	Abstellkämmerli (m)

V

English	Baseldütsch
vacant	frei
vacations	Feerie (pl)
vaccinate (verb)	impfe
vagina	Vagiina (f)
valley	Daal (n)
veal	Kalbfläisch (n)
vegan	vegaan
vegetables	Gmies (n)
vegetarian	vegedaarisch
vigorous	eneergisch
village	Dörfli (n)
vinegar	Essig (m)
violet	violett
virus	Wiirus (m)
visa	Wiisum (n)

W

English	Baseldütsch
waist	Dallie (f)
wake up call	Wegg-Delifon (m)
walk (verb)	lauffe
wall	Wand (f)
wallet	Boortmenee (n)
want (verb)	möchte /welle
ward	Abtäilig (f)
	Stazioon (f)
wardrobe	Gaarderoobe (f)
warehouse	Laagerhalle (f)
warm	waarm
wash (verb)	wäsche
washbasin	Brünneli (n)
	Lawaboo (n)
washing machine	Wöschmaschiine (f)
wasp	Wäschbi (n)
watch (verb)	luege
watermelon	Wassermeloone (f)
weather	Wätter (n)
weather report	Wätterbricht (m)
wedding	Hochzit (f)
wedding eve's party	Bolteroobe (m)
Wednesday	Mittwuch
week	Wuche (f)
weekend	Wuchenänd (n)
weep (verb)	briele / griine
	hüüle / schreie
welcome	Willkomme
well done (food)	duure
What ?	Waas ?
What for?	Für waas? / Werum?
When?	Wenn?
Where?	Woo?
whisper (verb)	flüschtere
white	wiss
white bread	Wiissbroot (n)
white fish	Felche (f)
white wine	Wisse (m)
	Wisswii (m)
Who with?	Mit wäm?
Who?	Wäär?
whole grain bread	Vollkoornbroot (n)
Why?	Werum?
wide	wiit
widow	Witwe (f)
widowed	verwitwet
widower	Witwer (m)
wife	Frau (f)
wild boar	Wildsau (f)

Dictionary

English	Baseldütsch
wind	Wind (m)
wind surfing	Windsöörfe
window	Fänschter (n)
wine	Wii (m)
wink (verb)	zwinggere
winter	Winter (m)
with / by (transport)	mit
withdraw (verb)	abheebe
without	ooni
wolf	Wolf (m)
women	Fraue
women's toilet	Daamedualette (pl)
	Fraueweezee (n)
wool	Wulle (f)
work (verb)	schaffe
worker	Aarbäiter (m)
	Aarbäitere (f)
	Biezer (m) / Biezere (f)
world	Wält (f)
worm	Wuurm (m)
worried	besoorgt
writing utensils	Schriibzüüg (n)

Y

English	Baseldütsch
yawn (verb)	gääne
year	Joor (n)
yellow	gääl
yes	joo
yesterday	geschter
yodelling	joodle
yoghurt	Jooguurt (n)
you	diir / du
young man	Buursch (m)
	junge Maa (m)
young woman	Froläin (n)
	jungi Frau (f)
youth hostel	Juugendheerbärg (f)

Z

English	Baseldütsch
zebra	Zeebra (n)
zero	null
zoo	Zoo (m) / Zolli

to the Baseldütsch-English Dictionary

Sali zämme - your Baseldütsch survival guide

Baseldütsch-English

A

aabe	down
aabegesetzt	discount
aabelaade	download (verb)
Aadler (m)	eagle
aaghängti Datei (f)	attachment
aaglegt	dressed
Aagstellte (m)	employee
Aagstellti (f)	employee
Aahang (m)	attachment
Aalaag (f)	attachment
Aakunft (f)	arrival
aalänge	touch (verb)
aaleege	dress (verb)
Aaloss (m)	event
aalütte	call (verb)
	telephone (verb)
Aamäise (f)	ant
aamälde	log in
Aarbäiter (m)	worker
Aarbäitere (f)	worker
Äärbeeri (n)	strawberry
Aarbetgääber (m)	employer
Aarbetgääbere (f)	employer
Aarbetsflechi (m)	desktop
Aarbetskolleeg (m)	colleague
Aarbetskolleegin (f)	colleague
aarbetsloos	unemployed
Aarbetsmappe (f)	briefcase
Äärdnussangge (m)	peanut butter
Aarm (m)	arm
Aaruef (m)	phone call
Aarzt (m)	doctor
Äärztin (f)	doctor
Aaschlagbrätt (n)	bulletin board
aasteggend	contagious
Aazuug (m)	dress / suit
Abdäilig (f)	department
abfaare	leave
Abfall (m)	trash
abheebe	withdraw (verb)
abluege	cheat (verb)
abmälde	log out
Abräis (f)	departure
Absänder/e (m/f)	sender's address
Abschiidsfescht (n)	farewell party
Abschnitt (m)	section
Abstellkämmerli (m)	utility room
Abszäss (m)	abscess
Abtäilig (f)	ward
Abwäschmaschiine (f)	dishwasher
Abzwiigig (f)	crossing
acht	eight
Achtung	be careful
achzää	eighteen
achzig	eighty
Adiöö (franz.: adieu)	Bye
Adrässbuech (n)	address book
Adrässe (f)	address
Aff (m)	monkey
Affeschwanz (m)	symbol '@'
Ägge (f)	neck
Äi (n)	egg
Äideggsli (n)	lizard
äigeständig	freelance
äinigi	some
äins	one
äinsaam	lonely
Äizimmerwoonig (f)	one-room flat
albe	sometimes
Aleergii (f)	allergy
alergisch uff ...	allergic to ...
Altbau (m)	old building
alte Maa (m)	old man
alti Frau (f)	old woman
am / an	at /on (vert. surface)
Ambulanz (f)	ambulance
amme	sometimes
Ample (f)	traffic light
Angge (m)	butter
Änglisch	English
ängschtlig	afraid / anxious
Änkel (m)	grandson
Änkelin (f)	granddaughter
antworte	reply
Aperitif (m)	appetizer
April (m)	April
är	he
Ardiggel (m)	article
Aschpiriin (n)	Aspirin
Aschtma (n)	asthma
ässe	eat (verb)
Assischtänt (m)	assistant
Assischtäntin (f)	assistant
Ässmänteli (n)	bib
Ässzimmer (n)	dining room
Ät (m)	symbol '@'
Attikawoonig (f)	attic flat
Aug (n)	eye
Augebraue (f)	eyebrow
Auguscht (m)	August
Auto (n)	car
Autobaan (f)	highway/motorway

B

B&B (n)	B&B
Baadwanne (f)	bath tub
Baadzimmer (n)	bathroom
Baanhoof (m)	train station
Baar (f)	bar
Bäär (m)	bear
Baar (n) / Baargäld (n)	cash
Bäärg (m)	mountain
Baarteer (n) (franz.: parterre)	ground floor
Bäch	bad luck
Bagge (m)	cheek
Baggoofe (m)	oven
Bäi (n)	leg
Bäiz (f)	restaurant
bald	soon

Dictionary

Balkon (m)	balcony	Blinddarmen-	appendicitis
Banaane (f)	banana	zündig (f)	
Bangg (f)	bank	blinzle	blink (verb)
Banggkonto (n)	bank account	Blitz (m)	lightning
Banggnoote (f)	banknote	blööd	stupid
Banggomaat (m)	cash machine	Bluemekool (m)	cauliflower
Bangsioonskasse (f)	pension fund	Bluet (n)	blood
Bapiirhandtuech (n)	paper towel	Bluetdrugg (m)	blood pressure
Bapiirkoorb (m)	trash	bluetig	rare (food)
Bass (m)	passport	Bluetzugger (m)	blood sugar
Bassä (n)	swimming pool	Blüschdier (n)	stuffed animal
(franz.: bassin)		Bluuse (f)	blouse
bätte	pray	Bolizei (f)	police
Bauele (f)	cotton	Bolizeiboschte (m)	police station
Baum (m)	tree	Bolteroobe (m)	hen night
Baumwulle (f)	cotton		wedding eve's party
Baziänt (m)	patient	Boode (m)	floor
Baziäntin (f)	patient	Boone (f)	beans
bedeggt	cloudy	Boonus (m)	bonus
Bedräff (m)	subject	boorde	board (verb)
bedrooge	betrayed	Boortmenee (n)	wallet
Beehaa (BH) (m)	bra	böös	angry
beesch	beige	Boscht (f)	post / post office
Begg (m)	bakery	boschte	buy (verb)
Beggerei (f)	bakery	Boschtkaarte (f)	debit card
bekannt	famous		postcard
Benziin (n)	petrol	Boschtläitzaal (f)	postal code
beriemt	famous	Böschtler (m)	postman
beriere	touch (verb)	Böschtlere (f)	postman
Berliiner (m)	jam doughnut	Boschtomaat (m)	cash machine
Berooter (f/m)	consultant	Boschtstämpel (m)	postage stamp
besoorgt	worried	brääglet	fried
Besprächig (f)	meeting	Breili (n)	baby food / mash
Bett (n)	bed	brenne	burn (verb)
Bettaazug (m)	bed cover	Bricht (m)	report
Bewäärbig (f)	job application	Brief (m)	letter
Bewäärbigs-	job interview	Briefdrääger (m)	postman
gsprööch (n)		Briefdrääger e (f)	postman
Bewilligung (f)	permit	Briefig (f)	exam
bewölkt	cloudy	Briefkaschte (m)	mailbox
bi	at	Briefmaargge (f)	stamp
Bibliotheek (f)	library	briele	cry / weep (verb)
Biebli (n)	baby boy	Briis (m)	fee / price
Biechergstell (n)	book shelves	Brimaarschuel (f)	elementary
Biecherlaade (m)	bookshop		primary school
Biene (f) / Bienli (n)	bee	Brimmeli (f)	elementary
Bier (n)	beer		primary school
Biezer (m)/ Biezere (f)	worker	Broggoli (m)	broccoli
Biilaag (f)	attachment	Bröntsch (m)	brunch
Biire (f)	pear	Broot (n)	bread
Bildschiirm (m)	screen	Bröötli (n)	roll
Billjee (n)	driving licence	Brootpfanne (f)	frying pan
	ticket	Broscht	cheers
bim / bi	by	Brotokoll (n)	minutes
bis	until	Brueder (m)	brother
Bitte	please	Bruef (m)	occupation
bitter	bitter	Brugg (f)	bridge
Blaan (m)	plan	Brülle (pl)	glasses
Blatz (m)	space	Brünneli (n)	washbasin
Blätzli (n)	steak	Bruscht (f)	breast / chest
blau	blue	Bruschtwaarze (f)	nipple
Bleistift (m)	pencil	bruun	brown
		bschisse	cheat (verb)
bsetzt	engaged		
Bsitzer (m)	owner		
Bsitzere (f)	owner		
bsoorge	buy (verb)		
Bstegg (n)	cutlery		
bstelle	order (verb)		
Bstellig (f)	purchase order		
Bueb (m)	boy		
Buech (n)	book		
Buechhandlig (f)	bookshop		
Buff (n)	argument		
büffle	drill (verb)		
Bunker (m)	bunker		
Bürschte (f)	brush		
Bus (m)	bus		
Busbaanhoof (m)	bus station		
Busbilljee (n)	bus ticket		
Buscheli (n)	baby		
Buschi(n)	baby		
Bushaltstell (f)	bus stop		
Butzfrau (f)	cleaner		
Butzmaa (m)	cleaner		
Buuch (m)	abdomen		
Buuchnaabel (m)	bellybutton		
Buuchwee (n)	stomach ache		
Büürli (n)	roll		
Büüro (n)	office		
Buursch (m)	young man		
Buuse (m)	breast / chest		
Buusi (n) / Buusle (f)	cat		

D

Dääfeli (n) / Dääfi (n)	candy
Daag (m)	day
Daageszitig (f)	newspaper
Daal (n)	valley
Daamedualette (pl)	women's toilet
Dablette (f)	pill
Dach (n)	roof
Dachkäänel (f)	gutter
Dachwoonig (f)	attic flat
Däigwaare (pl)	pasta
Däil (n)	section
Däilzit	part time
Däller (m)	plate
Dallie (f)	waist
Dämmerig (f)	dawn
Dämmerig (f)	dusk
danggbaar	grateful
Dangge	thank you
Dante (f)	aunt
danze	dance
Darleehe (n)	loan
Däsche (f)	bag / shopping bag
Dasse (f)	cup
dausig	one thousand
Deggi (f)	duvet
Delifon (n)	phone call
Delifon-	answering machine
beantworter (m)	
Delifonbuech (n)	telephone book
Delifonkaarte(f)	telephone card

Sali zämme - your Baseldütsch survival guide

Delifonkabiine (n)	public telephone
Delifonnummere	telephone number
Delifonnummere (f)	phone number
Delifonrächnig (f)	telephone bill
Delikatesselaade (m)	deli (catessen)
Dennisschue (pl)	tennis Shoes
Deo (m)	deodorant
Deppig (m)	carpet
Deppo (n)	deposit
depressiiv	depressed
der erschti Stock	first floor
der oberschti Stock	top floor
Desseer (m)	dessert
Dezämber (m)	December
Diäät (f)	diet
Diabeetes (f)	diabetes
diabeetisch	diabetic
Didschestiif (m) (franz.: digestive)	digestive
Dieb	thief
Diechli (n)	towel
Diefgaraasch (f)	basement garage
diefgfroore	frozen
Diefkieler (m)	freezer
Diiger (m)	tiger
diir	you
Ding (n)	thing
Diräggder (m)	director
Diräggdere (f)	director
Diräggdoorin (f)	director
Disch (m)	table
Dischduech (n)	table cloth
Dischset (n)	table mats
Disco (f)	discotheque
Dochter (f)	daughter
Doggder (m)	doctor
Doggdere (f)	doctor
Dollwuet (f)	rabies
Domaate (f)	tomato
Donner (m)	thunder
Donnschtig	Thursday
doo	here
Doodesaazäig (f)	obituary
doof	stupid
Doole (f)	jackdaw
Doon (m)	tuna
döörfe	may (verb)
döört	there
Doorte (f)	cake
Doppelbett (n)	double bed
Dörfli (n)	village
Draagduech (n)	baby sling
drei	three
drennt	separated
dringge	drink (verb)
drissig	thirty
drizää	thirteen
drogge	dry
Drooge (pl)	drugs
Dröpfli (pl)	drops
drugge	press / print
Drugger (m)	printer
Druthaan (m)	turkey
druurig	sad
du	you
Dualette (f) (franz.: Toilette)	toilet
Dualette-Papiir (n)	toilet paper
Dualettesache (pl)	toiletries
dunggels Broot (n)	brown bread
dunkel	dark
dur	through
Durchfall (m)	diarrhoea
Duschi (f)	shower
Duschmittel (n)	shower cream
Duschvoorhang (m)	shower curtain
düür	expensive
Düür (f)	door
duure	well done (food)
duusig	one thousand

E

e baar (weenigi)	a pair
e Fungg gää	call (verb)
e Fungg gää	telephone (verb)
e Milliarde (f)	one billion
e Million (f)	one million
Ee (f)	marriage
Eegli (m)	perch
Eesel (m)	donkey
Eezee-Kaarde (f) (EC-Kaarde)	debit card
Egge (m)	corner
Elefant (m)	elephant
Elektrogschäft (n)	electrical shop
elf	eleven
Ell(e)booge (m)	elbow
elläi-steehend	single
Empfang (m)	reception
eneergisch	vigorous
entlang	along
Entschuldigung	excuse me / sorry
enttüscht	disappointed
Enzündig (f)	infection
erfolgriich	successful
erscht	first
Erschti Hiilf (f)	first aid
erstuunt	amazed
Erwaggsene (m)	adult
Erwaggseni (f)	adult
Eschtrig (m)	attic
Espresso (m)	espresso
Essig (m)	vinegar
Exgüüsi (franz.: excusez)	excuse me

F

faad	tasteless
Faane (f)	flag
Faaneschwinge	swinging flags
Faargascht	passenger
Fäärnbedienig (f)	remote control
Fäärnsee (n)	television
Fäärnsee-bewilligung (f)	television licence
Faaruuswiis (m)	driving licence
Faasnacht (f)	Carnival
Fäld (n)	field
falte	fold
Familie	family
Familieschluuch (m)	family get together
Familiezämme-kunft (f)	family get together
Fänschter (n)	window
fantastisch	fantastic
Februaar (m)	February
Feerie (pl)	vacations
fein	delicious / fine
Felche (f)	white fish
Fescht (n)	party
Fieber (n)	fever
fiecht	humid
Finger (m)	finger
Fingernaagel (m)	fingernail
Fingge (pl)	slippers
Fisch (m)	fish
fische	fish (verb)
Fitness	fitness
Fitnessruum (m)	gym
Fläisch (n)	meat
Fliege (f)	fly
flüschtere	whisper (verb)
Fluss (m)	river
Fluugbilljee (n)	plane ticket
Fluugzüüg (n)	aeroplane
Forälle (f)	trout
Formulaar (n)	form
Fotteli (n) / Fotti (f)	photo
Frau (f)	wife
Fraue	women
Fraueweezee (n)	women's toilet
frei	vacant
frie	early
Frielig (m)	spring
Fritig	Friday
frittieert	deep fried
Froläin (n)	young woman
froo	joyful
fröölig	cheerful
Frucht (f)	fruit
Fründ (m)	boyfriend
Fründ/in (m/f)	friend
Fründin (f)	girlfriend
früsch	cool (temperature)
	fresh
Fuess (m)	foot
fuffzää	fifteen
fuffzig	fifty
Fuggs (m)	fox
Fülli (n)	fountain pen
fümf	five
Fümuar (n) (franz.: fumoir)	smoking area
Fungg (m)	phone call
für	for
Für waas?	What for?

Dictionary

Fuudi (n)	bottom	Gläiderknigge (f)	dress code	Grossunggle (m)	great uncle
Fuulaar (n)	scarf	Gläidervoorschrift (f)	dress code	Grossvatter (m)	grandfather
Füür	fire	Gläis (n)	track	Grövette (f)	shrimp
Füürstell (f)	grill area	Gläitschirm fliege	paragliding	Grüzzig (f)	crossing
Füürweer (f)	fire department	glangwiilt	bored	Gschäft (n)	office
		Glasse (n)	ice cream	gschiide	divorced
		(franz.: glace)		Gschiir (n)	dishes
G		glette	iron (verb)	Gschirr (n)	dinner service
		Glettiise (n)	iron	Gschmagg (m)	flavour
gää	give (verb)	glii	in a moment / soon	gschmaggloos	tasteless
Gaable (f)	fork	glotze	stare	Gschwindigkäits-	speed limit
gääl	yellow	Glüewii (m)	hot wine	begränzig (f)	
gääne	yawn (verb)	glügglig	happy	Gschwischterti (pl)	siblings
Gaarderoobe (f)	wardrobe	Glüggszaal (f)	lucky number	Gsellschaft (f)	society
gäärn haa	like (verb)	Gmies (n)	vegetables	Gsicht (n)	face
	love (verb)	gmietlig	cosy	Gsprööchsrundi (f)	talk show
Gaarte (m)	garden	Gnochebruch (m)	broken bone	gspunne	crazy
Gabbudschiino (m)	cappuccino	Gnöchel (m)	ankle	gstresst	stressed
Gabbuudscho (m)	cappuccino	Gnöi (n)	knee	Gsundhäit	health
(ital.: Cappuccino)		Gnopf (m)	button	guet	fine / good
Gäiss (f)	goat	goldig	gold	Guete Moorge	good morning
Gäld (n)	money	Gomfi (f)	jam	Guete Nomidaag	good afternoon
Gäld inweschtiere	invest money	Gomfiglaas (n)	jam jar	Gueten Oobe	good evening
Gäld verdiene	earn money	Gonsiersch	concierge	Guetnacht-	bedtime story
Gäldautomat (m)	cash machine	*(franz.: concierge)*		Gschichtli (n)	
Gäldüüberwiisig (f)	postal money order	goo	go (verb)	Gugge (f)	shopping bag
Gäms (f) / Gämsi (n)	chamois	goorbse	burp	Güggel (m)	rooster
Gang (m)	hallway	göörbsle	burp (baby)	Güggeli (n)	chicken
Garaasch (f)	garage	Goschdüüm (n)	suit	Gummi (m)	condom / eraser
(franz.: garage)		graad	in a moment		rubber
Gebäck (n)	pastry	graadi Zaale	even numbers	gumpe	jump (verb)
Geböid (n)	building	graaduss	straight on	Güppli (n)	champagne (glass)
Gebüür (f)	fee	Graage (m)	collar	Gürtel (m)	belt
Gebuurtsdaag	birthday	Grampf (m)	cramp	Guurt (m)	belt
Gebuurtsdaags-	birthday party	grangg	sick	Guusäng (m)	cousin
Paarti		Granggekasse (f)	health insurance	Guusiine (f)	cousin
geege	against	Granggenauti (m)	ambulance	Guweer (n)	envelope
geege	into	Granggepflääger (m)	nurse	*(franz.: Couvert)*	
Geegemittel (n)	antidote	Grangge-	nurse	Gwändli (n)	suit
geegenüüber	across from	schweschter (f)		Gwitter (n)	thunderstorm
	opposite	Gränze (f)	frontier / border	Gwüürz (pl)	condiment
Geegewaart (f)	now / present	Grätsch (n)	gossip		
Genäämigung (f)	permit	Gratulazioon	congratulations	**H**	
Geografii (f)	geography	grau	grey		
Gepäck (n)	luggage	Grawatte (f)	tie	haa	have (verb)
geschter	yesterday	Greeme (f)	cream	Hääfelischuel (m)	kindergarten
Ghäimnummerä (f)	code	grien	green	Haagel (m)	hail
ghüüroote	married	Griezi	hello	haagle	hail (verb)
Gift (n)	poison	griiffe	grab (verb)	Haane (m)	faucet / tap
giggerig	horny	griine	cry / weep (verb)	Häärd (m)	stove
Giigampfi (f)	swing	grilieert	grilled	Häärdöpfel (m)	potatoes
Gimmeli (n)	baccalaureate	Grill (m)	grill	Häärz (n)	heart
	school	Grillfescht (n)	barbecue	häärzig	lovely
Gimmeli (n)	gymnasium (school)	Grippe (f)	flu	Hächt (m)	pike
Gimnaasium (n)	baccalaureate	Groggedill (n)	crocodile	häi	home
	school / gymnasium	grööschtet	roasted	Häilmittel (n)	medicine
	(school)	gross	big / large	häiss	hot
Gipfel (m)	peak	Grossdante (f)	great aunt	Häissi Milch (f)	hot milk
Gipfeli (n)	croissant	Grossdochter (f)	granddaughter	Häissi Schoggi (f)	hot chocolate
Glaas (n)	glass	Grosseltere (pl)	grandparents	häiter	cheerful
gläi	short / small	Grosskind (n)	grandchild	Halbbangsioon (f)	half board
Gläid (n)	dress	Grossmueter (f)	grandmother	halbduure	medium (meat)
Gläider (pl)	clothing	Grosssoon (m)	grandson	häll	clear
Gläiderbüügel (m)	hanger				

Sali zämme - your Baseldütsch survival guide

Hals (m)	throat
Halsduech (n)	scarf
Hand (f)	hand
Handdäschli (n)	purse
Händedroggner (m)	hand dryer
Händel (m)	argument
Handgreeme (f)	hand cream
Händi (n)	cell phone / mobile phone
händle	argue (verb)
Handöörgeli (n)	Swiss accordion
Händsche (pl)	gloves
hässig	furious
Hauptspiis (f)	main course
heebe	hold (verb)
heerlig	delicious
Heftli (n)	magazine
Hemmli (n)	shirt
Herbscht (m)	autumn
Herredualette (pl)	men's toilet
Herusgääber (m)	editor
Herusgääbere (f)	editor
hetero(sexuell)	heterosexual
Hienerhutt (f)	goose bumps
Hiilfe (f)	help
Hiirnerschütterig (f)	concussion
Himbeeri (n)	raspberry
hinder	behind
Hinderleegig (f)	deposit
Hirsch (m)	deer
Hitz (f)	heat
Hochzit (f)	wedding
Höischnuppe (m)	hay fever
homo(sexuell)	homosexual
Hööemässer (m)	altimeter
Hoonig (m)	honey
Hoor (pl)	hair
hööre	hear
Hoose (f)	trousers
Hotelhalle (f)	lobby
hübsch	pretty
Huen (n)	chicken
hueschte	cough (verb)
Huet (m)	hat
Huft / Hüfte (f)	hip
Hülsefrücht (pl)	legumes
Hummer (m)	lobster
Humoor (m)	humour
Hund (m)	dog
hundert	one hundred
hundertdausig	hundred thousand
hundertduusig	hundred thousand
Hutt (f)	skin
hütt(e)	today
Hüügel (m)	hill
hüüle	cry / weep (verb)
Huus (n)	house
Huusbsitzer (m)	home owner
Huusbsitzere (f)	home owner
Huusglogge (f)	doorbell
Huusiiweiigs-Paarti (f)	housewarming party
Huusnummere (f)	house number
Huus-Uffgoobe (pl)	homework

I

ich	I
Idiottehüügel (m)	easy hill to ski
iifersüchtig	envious / jealous
ligang (m)	entrance
ligangshalle (f)	lobby
iigschriibene Brief (m)	registered letter
iigschriibeni Boscht (f)	registered mail
iikaufe	shopping (verb)
likaufszentrum (n)	shopping centre
likaufszentrum (n)	supermarket
likomme (n)	income
iilogge	log in
li-Meil (n)	e-mail
iiräise	immigrate (verb)
Iis	ice
Iiskaschte (m)	fridge
Iistellhalle (f)	garage
ii-tschegge	check in
im Momänt	now
im Momänt	present
Imbiss-Stand (m)	take away
impfe	vaccinate (verb)
in	in / into
in Zuekumft	future
Inland-Noochrichte (pl)	national news
Innerstadt (f)	city
Inseggt (n)	insect
Insle (f)	island
Intensiivstazioon (f)	intensive care
Internetaaschluss	internet connection
Inweschtizioon (f)	investment
irgendöppis	anything
irgendwie	somehow
irr	crazy

J

Jagge (f)	jacket
Januaar (m)	January
jetz	now / present
joo	yes
joodle	yodelling
Jooguurt (n)	yoghurt
joomere	complain
Joor (n)	year
Joordausig (n)	millennium
Joorduusig (n)	millennium
Jooreszit (f)	season
Joorhundert (n)	century
Jubilääum	anniversary
Juli (m)	July
junge Maa (m)	young man
jungi Frau (f)	young woman
Juni (m)	June
Junte (f)	skirt
Juugendheerbärg (f)	youth hostel

K

Kaabelfäärnsee (n)	cable TV
Kääfer (m)	beetle
kääre	argue (verb)
Kaarte (f)	map
Kääs (m)	cheese
Kaater (m)	cat
Kaffi (n)	cafe / coffee bar
Kaffi Greem (m) (franz.: Café crème)	coffee (w/cream)
Kaffiklatsch (m)	coffee party
Kaffikränzli (n)	coffee party
Kaffipause (f)	coffee break
Kalbfläisch (n)	veal
Käller (m)	basement / cellar
kalt	cold
Kämping (n)	camping
Kanaal (m)	channel
Kantiine (f)	canteen
Kantoon (m)	county
Kappe (f)	cap
Kaschte (m)	closet
Kassierer (m)	cashier
Kassierere (f)	cashier
Kathedraale (f)	Cathedral
Katz (f)	cat
kauffe	buy (verb)
Kemmi (n)	chimney
kiel	cool (temperature)
Kiino (n)	cinema
Kiirsi (n)	cherry
Kilo (n)	kilo
Kinder	children
Kinderaarzt (m)	pediatrician
Kinderäärztin (f)	pediatrician
Kinderbett (n)	cot
Kinderbett (n)	crib
Kindergaarte (m)	kindergarten
Kinderwaage (m)	pram
Kinderwaage (m)	stroller
Kinderzimmer (n)	children's room
Kindsgi (m)	kindergarten
Kirche (f)	church
Kischte (f)	box
Klatsch (m)	gossip
klatsche	gossip (verb)
Kliima (n)	climate
Kliinik (f)	clinic
Knooblauch (m)	garlic
kocht	boiled
Komferänz (f)	conference
Komissioon (f)	commission
Kondoom (n)	condom
könne	can (verb)
Kontinänt (m)	continent
Konzäärt (n)	concert
koo	come (verb)
Kood (m)	code
Köörpermilch (f)	body lotion
kooscher	kosher
Kopf (m)	head
Kopfsalaat (m)	lettuce

Dictionary

Kopfwee (n)	headache	Leerling (m)	apprentice	Meer (n)	sea
kopiere	copy	lesbisch	lesbian	Meeresfrücht (pl)	seafood
Koschte (pl)	costs	liebe	love (verb)	Meersi *(franz.: merci)*	thank you
Krabbe (f)	crab	Lift (m)	lift	Meersöili (n)	guinea pig
Kreditkaarde (f)	credit card	Liibli (n)	T-shirt	Meerz (m)	march
Krippe (f)	daycare	Liinduech (n)	sheet	Meil (n)	e-mail
Kuchi (f)	kitchen	Liine (f)	linen	Mensa (f)	canteen
Kuchikäschtli (n)	kitchen cupboard	lila	lilac	Mesonett-Woonig (f)	two-level flat
Kue (f)	cow	Limoone (f)	lime	*(franz.: Maisonnette)*	
Kueche (m)	cake	linggs	left	Metzgerei (f)	butcher's shop
Kulli (m)	biro / pen	Linse (pl)	lentils	mied	sleepy
Kultuur (f)	culture	Liter (m)	litre	miesse	must (verb)
Kund (m)	customer	Löffel (m)	spoon	Mieter (m)	tenant
Kundin (f)	customer	Löi (m)	lion	Mietere (f)	tenant
Küngel (m)	rabbit	lokaali Nöiigkäite (pl)	local news	Mietwoonig (f)	rental flat
Kunscht (f)	art	Lokaal-Noochrichte (pl)	local news	Mikrowälle (f)	microwave
kurz	short	Loon (m)	salary	Milch (f)	milk
kurzeermlig	short sleeves	loose	listen (verb)	Milchkaffi (m)	coffee with milk
kurzi Hoose (pl)	shorts	lösche	cancel (verb)	mild	mild
Kuss	kiss	luege	look (verb)	minus	minus
Küssi (n)	pillow		see (verb)	Minute (f)	minute
kuul	cool (feeling)		watch (verb)	Mischtküübel (m)	rubbish bin
Kuurs (m)	course	Luftboscht (f)	airmail	mit	with / by (transport)
		Luftschutzkäller (m)	bunker	Mit wäm?	Who with?

L

		Luggs (m)	lynx	Mittag (m)	midday
		luschtig	funny	Mittag (m)	noon
		lutsche	lick	Mittagspause (f)	lunch break
Lääbe	life			mittel	medium (size)
Lääbere (f)	liver			mittelgross	medium (size)

M

Lääbesmittel (pl)	groceries			Mittwuch	Wednesday
Lääbespaartner (m)	partner			möchte	want (verb)
Lääbespaartnere (f)	partner	Maa (m)	husband	Möisebussard (m)	buzzard
Laade (m)	shop / store	Maage (m)	stomach	Momänt (m)	moment
läädele	shopping (verb)	Määl (n)	flour	momäntaan	now / present
Lääder (n)	leather	Määntig	Monday	Moode (f)	fashion
Laagerhalle (f)	warehouse	Maarder (m)	marten	mööge	like (verb)
lääse	read (verb)	Maargeriine (f)	margarine	Moolzite (pl)	meals
Laboor (n)	laboratory	Maargge (f)	brand / stamp	Moonet (m)	month
lache	laugh	Maduur (f)	baccalaureate	Moorge (m)	morning
lächle	smile		degree	Moorgedämmerig (f)	dawn
Lachs (m)	salmon	Maduur (f)	maturity diploma	moorn	tomorrow
Läischtigsbewäärtig (f)	appraisal	Mäi (m)	May	Moschee (f)	mosque
Lamm (n)	lamb	Mäinig (f)	opinion	Moscht (m)	petrol
Lämpe (plur.)	argument	Mäis (m)	corn	mozze	complain
Land (n)	country	Mäiskolbe (m)	corn on the cob	Mueter (f)	mother
lande	land	Mäiteli (n)	baby girl	Mugge (f)	mosquito
Ländler (m)	Swiss trad. music	Mäitli (n)	girl	Mungg (m)	marmot
lang	long	Mänätscher (m)	manager	Münschter (n)	Cathedral
länge	grab (verb)	Mänätschere (f)	manager	Münz (n) / Münze (pl)	small change
langeermlig	long sleeves	Manderiinli (n)	tangerine	Münze (f)	coin
langlauffe	cross country skiing	Männer	men	Museeum (n)	museum
		Männerweezee	men's toilet	Muul (n)	mouth
Läppi (m)	laptop	männgisch	sometimes	Muurmeldier (n)	marmot
Läptop (m)	laptop	männgmool	sometimes	Muurmeli (n)	marmot
Latte Maggiaaddo (n)	latte macchiato	Mantel (m)	coat	Muus (f) / Müüsli (f)	mouse
(ital.: latte macchiato)		Mappe (f)	briefcase	Muusig (f)	music
Laubflägge (pl)	freckles	marinieert	marinated		
lauffe	walk (verb)	Massaasch (f)	massage		
Lawaboo (n)	washbasin	*(franz.: massage)*			

N

Lawiine	avalanche	Mässer (n)	knife	nääbe	beside / next to
leedig	single	Maudi (m)	cat	Nääbel (m)	fog
leere	learn (verb)	Medikamänt	medicine	Naagel (m)	nail
	teach (verb)	mee	more	Naame (m)	name
Leerere (f) / Leerer (m)	teacher	meedium	medium (meat)		

153

Sali zämme - your Baseldütsch survival guide

Naase (f)	nose	Paarti (f)	party	reklamiere	complain
Naashorn (n)	rhinoceros	Paartner (m)	partner	reserviere	reserve (verb)
Nacht (f)	night	Paartnere (f)	partner	Ressepsion (f)	reception
Näi	no	Päckli (n)	packet	(franz.: réception)	
Näilen (n)	nylon	Parasit (m)	parasite	Ressepzionischt (m)	receptionist
näime	somewhere	Pariiser (m)	condom	Ressepzionischtin (f)	receptionist
Natel (n)	cell phone	Pariiserbroot (n)	baguette	Rezäpt (n)	prescription
	mobile phone	Passaschier (m)	passenger	Riebli (n)	carrots
Neffe (m)	nephew	Pause (f)	break / recess	Riis (m)	rice
Nessesseer (n)	toiletry bag	Peenis (m)	penis	Riisegrövette (f)	prawns
(franz.: nécessaire)		Peperooni (f)	pepper	Rindfläisch (n)	beef
Nichte (f)	niece	Perron (n)	platform	Ritti (f)	swing
Nichtraucher	no smoking	Pfanne (f)	pan	Rogg (m)	skirt
niidisch	envious	Pfiffli (n)	penis	roo	raw
Niilpfäärd (n)	hippopotamus	Pfläschterli (n)	Band-aid	roosa	pink
noch	after	Pflichteheft (n)	job description	root	red
Nöibau (m)	new building	Pfund (n)	pound	root wärde	blush (verb)
nöime	somewhere	Piggnigg (n)	picnic	Roote (m) / Rootwii (n)	red wine
Nomidaag (m)	afternoon	Pille (f)	pill	Ross (n)	horse
Noochbere (pl)	neighbours	Pinnkood (m)	code	rueig	quiet
Noochrichte (pl)	news	Pissuar (n)	urinal	rueigi Laag (f)	quiet area
Nootfall (m)	emergency	(franz.: Pissoir)		Rugge (m)	back
Nootuffnaam (f)	emergency room	plus	plus	Ruggsagg (m)	backpack
Nootussgang (m)	emergency exit	Polijeschter (m)	polyester	Ruggsagg (m)	rucksack
Novämber (m)	november	Praktikant (m)	trainee	Ruum (m)	space
Nöwöö (m)	nephew	Praktikantin (f)	trainee		
Nuggi (m)	dummy / pacifier	Praxis (f)	doctor's surgery		
null	zero	Presentazioon (f)	presentation	**S**	
nüt	nothing	Profi (m/f)	professional		
nüün	nine	Profitt (m)	profit	S duet mer läid.	sorry
nüünzää	nineteen	Promi (m)	celebrity	s goot eso	so-so
nüünzig	ninety	Proviant (m)	provisions	saage	say (verb)
		Pult (n)	desk	Sach (f)	thing
		pünggtlig	on time	sächzää	sixteen
		Punnsch (m)	punch	sächzig	sixty
				Saggmässer (n)	Swiss army knife
O				säggs	six
		Q		Säiffi (f)	soap
Oberdail (n)	top			Salaami (m)	salami
Oberschiine (f)	eggplant	Quaark (m)	curd cheese	Saläär (n)	salary
offe	open (adj.)	Qualifikazioon (f)	appraisal	Salaat (m)	salad
oggse	drill (verb)			Salaatsoosse (f)	dressing
Oggtoober (m)	October			sälbständig	self-employed
Ojee	sorry	**R**		Sali / Salli	hi
Oliivenööl (n)	olive oil			salzig	salty
Oobe (m)	evening	Raadio (m)	radio	sammle	collect (verb)
Oobedämmerig (f)	dusk	Rääge (m)	rain	Samschtig	Saturday
Oobegläid (n)	evening dress	räägne	rain (verb)	Sändwidsch (n)	sandwich
ooni	without	Raam (m)	cream	Saniteet (f)	ambulance
Oopere (f)	opera	raase	drive (fast)	Santee	cheers
Oor (n)	ear	Raase (m)	lawn	Sässelilift (m)	chair lift
Operazioon (f)	operation	Raasemäier (m)	lawnmower	Satellit (m)	satellite
Öpfel (m)	apple	Rächnig (f)	invoice	Satelliteschüssle (f)	satellite dish
öppe / öppedie	sometimes	rächts	right	Sau (f)	pig
öpper	somebody	Radaar (m)	speed camera	Saufläisch (n)	pork
öppis	something	räise	travel (verb)	schaad	shame
orangsch	orange (colour)	Raschtblatz (m)	service area	Schaal (m)	scarf
Orangsche (f)	orange	Raschtstett (f)	service area	Schaale (f)	coffee with milk
Orangschegomfi (f)	marmalade	Rasierklinge (f)	razor blades		suit
Ozeaan (m)	ocean	rätsche	gossip (verb)	schaarf	spicy
		Raucheregge (m)	smoking area	Schachtle (f)	box
		reduziert	discount	schaffe	work (verb)
P		Ree (n)	roe deer	Schalter (m)	counter
		reede	speak	Schampo (n)	shampoo
Paark (m)	park				
Paarkblatz (m)	parking area				

Dictionary

schanze	drill (verb)	schwarzes Brätt (n)	bulletin board	spitz	horny
Schätzli	treasure (little)	Schweschter (f)	sister	Spoort (m)	sports
Scheff (m)	boss	Schwiigerdochter (f)	daughter-in-law	spoot	late
(franz.: chef)		Schwiigermueter (f)	mother-in-law	springe	jump (verb)
Scheffin (f)	boss	Schwiigersoon (m)	son-in-law	Sprützi (f)	injection
Schegg (m)	cheque	Schwiigervatter (m)	father-in-law	Stääge (f)	stairs
Schegg (pl)	travelers cheques	Schwiinigs (n)	pork	staarre	stare
schigge	send (verb)	Schwimmbaad (n)	swimming pool	Staat (m)	state
Schii (m)	ski	schwimme	swim (verb)	Stadt (f)	city / town
schiifaare	skiing	schwinge	Swiss wrestling	Stadtblaan (f)	map
Schiileerer (m)	ski instructor	Schwizer Frangge (m)	Swiss franc	Stadtblaan (m)	city map
Schiileerere (f)	ski instructor	Schwizerdütsch	Swiss German	Stäibogg (m)	European ibex
Schiilift (m)	ski lift	Schwoobekääfer (f)	cockroach	Stange (f)	draft beer
Schiischue (m)	ski boot	Schwööbli (n)	roll	Stazioon (f)	ward
Schiischuel (f)	ski school	Schwooer (m)	brother-in-law	Stegger (m)	plug
Schildgrot (f)	turtle	Schwöögere (f)	sister-in-law	Stier (m)	bull
Schingge (m)	ham	schwuul	gay	Stiirne (f)	forehead
Schlaagziile (pl)	headlines	see	see (verb)	stille	nurse (verb)
schlächt	bad	See (m)	lake	Stögg (pl)	ski poles
Schlange (f)	snake	Seggredäär (m)	secretary	Stoore (m)	sunshade
schlapp	sleepy	Seggredäärin (f)	secretary	Strääl (m)	comb
schliesse	close (verb)	Sek (f)	secondary school	Strampelhoose (m)	sleeper
Schloofdablette (f)	sleeping pill	Sekundaarschuel (f)	high school	Strand (m)	beach
schloofe	sleep (verb)	Sekunde (f)	second	Striit (m)	argument
Schloofloosikäit (f)	insomnia	sentimentaal	sentimental	stritte	argue (verb)
schlööfrig	sleepy	Septämber (m)	September	Strooss (f)	street
Schloofzimmer (n)	bedroom	Service (n)	dinner service	Strümpf (pl)	stockings
Schlumbi (n)	roll	Serviette (f)	napkin	Stuel (m)	chair
Schlüssel (m)	key	sexi	sexy	Stüggli (pl)	pastry
Schmäärze (pl)	pain	sibzää	seventeen	Stund (f)	hour
schmäärzhaft	painful	sibzig	seventy	Stuube (f)	lounge
Schmäärzmittel (n)	pain killer	sich beklaage	complain	Stuudio (n)	studio
schmegge	smell	sich d Naase butze	blow one's nose	Stüüre (pl)	taxes
Schminkzüüg (n)	make-up	sich drenne	separate (verb)	Stuurm (m)	storm
schmuuse	kiss (verb)	Sicherhäit (f)	security	Summer (m)	summer
Schnägg (m)	slug	siess	sweet	Summersprosse (pl)	freckles
schnäll	hurry	sii	they	Sunne (f)	sun
Schnaps (m)	spirit	siibe	seven	Sunnedach (n)	sunshade
Schnee (m)	snow	Siide (f)	silk	sunnig	sunny
Schneeschue lauffe	snow shoeing	Siinagooge (f)	synagogue	Sunntig	Sunday
Schnitzel (n)	steak	Siirup (m)	syrup	Supermäärt (m)	supermarket
Schobbe (m)	baby bottle	silbrig	silver	suuge	suck
schöön	beautiful	singel	single	suur	sour
Schoorts (pl)	shorts	Sitzig (f)	meeting	suure Moscht (m)	cider
schreie	weep (verb)	SMS (n)	text message		
Schriibtisch (m)	desktop	snööbe	board (verb)	**T**	
Schriibzüüg (n)	writing utensils	so soo la laa	so-so		
Schteegg (n)	steak	Sogge (pl)	socks	Talk Show (engl.)	talk show
Schue (pl)	shoes	Soon (m)	son	Tampon (m)	tampon
Schuel (f)	school	spaare	save (verb)	Tankstell (f)	petrol station
Schuelhuus (n)	school	Spaarkonto (n)	savings account	Techniker (m)	technician
Schuelsagg (m)	satchel / school	Spägg (m)	bacon	Technikere (f)	technician
	bag	Späm	spam	Tee (m)	tea
	backpack	Spidaal (n)	hospital	Teelöffeli (n)	teaspoon
Schultere (f)	shoulder	Spiegel (m)	mirror	Temperatuur (f)	temperature
Schüp (m)	skirt	spigge	cheat (verb)	Termiin (m)	appointment
Schüssle (f)	bowl	Spiil (n)	game	Terrasse (f)	terrace
schutte	play football	spiile	gamble (verb)	Tescht (m)	test
schüttle	shake		play (verb)	Theaater (n)	theatre
Schuublaade (f)	drawer	Spiiskarte	menu	Tiini (m)	teenager
schüüch	shy	Spiiswaage (m)	dining car	Tömbler (m)	tumble drier
schwaarz	black	Spinaat (m)	spinach	Tooscht (m)	toast
schwanger	pregnant	Spinne (f)	spider	traatsche	gossip (verb)

Sali zämme - your Baseldütsch survival guide

Tratsch (m)	gossip
Tschäpper (m)	cap
Tschau / Tschüss	Bye
Tschiins (pl)	jeans
Tschob (m)	occupation
Turischt (m)	tourist
Turischtin (f)	tourist

U

über	above / across / over
überrascht	surprised
überwiise	transfer (verb)
uff	on (horiz. surface)
Uff Wiiderluege	Bye
Uff Wiidersee	Bye
Uffdraag (m)	purchase order
uffe	up
Uffenthalts- genäämigung (f)	residence permit
Uffgoobe (pl)	homework
uffgreggt	excited
uffgstellt	cheerful
uffmache	open (verb)
um	around
umaarme	hug
umfalle / umfliege	fall down (verb)
umgheie	fall down (verb)
umme	past
und	plus
under	beneath / under
Underhaltig (f)	entertainment
Underhoose (f)	panties
Underschrift (f)	signature
Underwösch (f)	underwear
Unggle (m)	uncle
Unglüggszaal (f)	unlucky number
ungraadi Zaale	odd numbers
Uni (f)	university
Unifoorm (f)	uniform
Universideet (f)	university
unzwunge	business casual
us	from
ussgää	spend (verb)
Ussgang (m)	exit
Ussländer (m)	foreigner
Ussländere (f)	foreigner
Ussland-Noochrichte (pl)	international news
usslogge	log out
ussräise	emigrate (verb)
Ussrüschtig (f)	equipment
Uss-stellig (f)	exhibition
uss-tschegge	check out
Ussverkauf	on sale
Üüberstunde (pl)	overtime
Uurgrossmueter (f)	great grandmother
Uurgrossvatter (m)	great grandfather
uusdroggne	dry out
uuszie	move out (verb)

V

Vagiina (f)	vagina
Vatter (m)	father
vegaan	vegan
vegedaarisch	vegetarian
veräinzelti	a pair
Verband (m)	bandage
verbii	verbii
Verbilligung (f)	discount
Verbindig (f)	connection
verbrennt	burned
verbutze	spend (verb)
Verdraag (m)	contract
vergange	past
Vergangehäit (f)	past
vergänggerle	spend (verb)
vergiftet	poisoned
Verhietigsmittel (n)	contraceptive
verkauffe	sell (verb)
Verkeltig (f)	cold
Verköiffer (m)	salesperson
Verköiffere (f)	salesperson
Verletzig (f)	injury
verliebt	in love
verlobt	engaged
Verlobte (m)	fiancé
Verlobti (f)	fiancée
Verluscht (m)	loss
Vermieter (m)	landlord
Vermietere (f)	landlord
verruggt	crazy
versalze	over salted
Versicherig (f)	insurance
Versicherigs-Nummere (f)	insurance number
Verspöötig (f)	delay
Vertäilerli (m)	digestive
Verwaltig (f)	estate agency
Verwaltigsroot (m)	board of directors
Verwandti (pl)	relatives
verwitwet	widowed
verzolle	declare (at customs)
verzwiiflet	desperate
vier	four
vierzää	fourteen
vierzig	forty
viil	many / much
violett	violet
Vip (m) (VIP)	celebrity
vo	from / of
Vo woo?	from where?
Vollbangsioon (f)	full board
Vollkoornbroot (n)	whole grain bread
Vollziit	full time
Voogel (m)	Bird
voor	in front of
Voorhäng (pl)	curtains
Voorruum (m)	lobby
Voorspiis (f)	starter
Vorwaal (f)	area code

W

Wääg (m)	footpath / path
Wääie (f)	pie
Wäär?	Who?
Wäärbig (f)	advertising
wäärde	become (verb)
Wäärig (f)	currency
waarm	warm
Waas ?	What ?
wäffele	complain
Wäggselkuurs (f)	exchange rate
Wägwiiser (m)	direction sign
Wald (m)	forest
Wält (f)	world
Wand (f)	wall
wandere	hiking
Wanderschue (pl)	hiking shoes
Wanderwääg (m)	hiking path
Wäntele (f)	bug
Wäschbi (n)	wasp
Wäschblätz (m)	towel
wäsche	wash (verb)
Wassermeloone (f)	watermelon
Wätter (n)	weather
Wätterbricht (m)	forecast
Wätterbricht (m)	weather report
Wee	pain
weenig	few
weeniger	less
Weezee (n)	toilet
Weezee-Papiir (n)	toilet paper
Wegg-Delifon (m)	wake up call
welle	want (verb)
Welo (n)	bicycle
Wenn?	When?
Werum?	What for?
Werum?	Why?
Wie lang?	how long?
Wie viil?	how many? / how much?
Wie?	how?
Wienacht	Christmas
Wiggeldisch (n)	changing table
Wii (m)	wine
wiiderhoole	repeat
Wiirtschaft (n)	restaurant
Wiirus (m)	virus
Wiissbroot (n)	white bread
Wiisum (n)	visa
wiit	wide
Wildsau (f)	wild boar
Willkomme	welcome
Wimpere (pl)	eyelash
Wind (m)	wind
Windle (pl)	diapers
Windle (pl)	nappies
Windsöörfe	wind surfing
Winter (m)	winter
wisawii	across from opposite
wiss	white
Wisse (m)	white wine

Dictionary

Wisswii (m)	white wine	Zaan (m)	tooth	Znüüni (m)	snack (morning)		
witerläite	forward	Zaanbaschta (f)	toothpaste	Zoll (m)	customs		
Witwe (f)	widow	Zaanbürschtli (n)	toothbrush	Zolli	zoo		
Witwer (m)	widower	zaane	teeth (verb)	Zoo (m)	zoo		
Witz (m)	joke	Zaanwee	toothache	zruggschriibe	reply		
witzig	funny	zämme	together	zue (adj.)	closed		
Wo aane?	to where?	Zander (m)	jack salmon	zuedue	close (verb)		
Wolf (m)	wolf	Zäpfli (n)	suppositories	zueheebe	cover		
Woo?	Where?	zaubere (Verb)	magic (verb)	Zuekumft (f)	future		
Woog (f)	scales	Zauberei (f)	magic	zuekümftig	future		
Wösch (f)	laundry	Zeebra (n)	zebra	zuemache	close (verb)		
Wöschdaag (m)	laundry day	Zeeche (m)	toe	Zugbilljee (n)	train ticket		
Wöschkorb (m)	laundry basket	Zeechenaagel (m)	toenail	Zugger (m)	diabetes		
Wöschkuchi (f)	laundry room	zer Zit	now	Zugger (m)	sugar		
Wöschmaschiine (f)	washing machine	zer Zit	present	zuhande vo	care of		
Wöschmittel (n)	detergent	zfriide	joyful	zum Mitnää	take away (verb)		
Wöschblaan (m)	laundry schedule	Zigerette	cigarette	Zunge (f)	tongue		
Wöschsagg (m)	laundry bag	Ziibele (f)	onion	Zuug (m)	train		
Wöschzäine (f)	laundry basket	Zimmer (n)	room	Züügnis (n)	report card		
Wuche (f)	week	Zimmermäitli (f)	room service	Züügnis (n)	school report		
Wuchenänd (n)	weekend	Zimmer-Seerwis (m)	room service	Zvieri (m)	snack (afternoon)		
Wulle (f)	wool	Zins (m)	interest	zwäi	two		
Wurscht (f)	sausage	Zischtig	Tuesday	zwäidausig	two thousand		
Wuurm (m)	worm	Zitig (f)	newspaper	zwäiduusig	two thousand		
		Zitroone (f)	lemon	zwäihundert	two hundred		
Z		Ziviilstand (m)	marital status	Zwäizimmer Woonig(f)	two-room flat		
		Zmittag (m)	lunch	zwanzig	twenty		
		Zmittagässe (n)	lunch	Zwilling (pl)	twins		
z Fuess	on foot	Zmoorge (m)	breakfast	zwinggere	wink (verb)		
zää	ten	Znacht (m)	dinner	zwölf	twelve		
zää Joor (f)	decade	Znacht (m)	supper	zwüsche	between		
zaale	pay (verb)	Znachtässe (n)	dinner				
Zaalig (f)	payment						

The End
(SOODELI, DAS WÄÄRS)

Sali zämme - your Baseldütsch survival guide

Sali zämme - your Baseldütsch survival guide

Index

A

Age 93
Alcohol 49
Alemannic tribes 6
Animals 108–109
   Alpine Wildlife 108
Articles 132–133
   Definite Articles 132
   Indefinite Articles 132

B

Babies 92
Banking. *See* Money
Basel Dishes 51
Bread 50
Bugs. *See* Insects
BVB 74-75
   BVB ticket machine 75

C

Clothes 70–71
   Accessories 71
   Clothing Materials 71
Cold Drinks 48
Colours 107
   Baseldütsch Idioms 107
Computer 40–41
Confusions 126–129
Consonants 18
Customs 66

D

Dairy Products 50

Days of the Week 112
Dialects 6–7
Dialäggtgmisch 5
Diets 53
Diglossia 8
Directions 78–79
Dress Code 36
Drinks 46, 48–49
   Cold Drinks 48–49
   Hot Drinks 48–49
   Typical Drinks 49

E

Education 105
E-mail 40–41
Emergency 64
Emotions 61–63
Entertainment 86–89
   Basel Traditions 89
Estate Agent 100–101
Exchange Office. *See* Money

F

Family 90–91
   Family Relations 91
   Marital Status 90
Flat 98–99
Flavours 52
Food 46–53
   Places to Eat 53
French influences 10
Fruits 52

Sali zämme - your Baseldütsch survival guide

G

General Terms 106
  Generic Words 106
  Measurements 106
  Quantity 106
  Time 106
Geography 83
Greetings 20–23
  Hello (Formal) 20
  Hello (Informal) 21
  Politeness 23

H

Health 54–60
  Health Problems 57
  Health Remedies 57
High German 8–9,15
History of the Dialects 6–7
Hobbies. *See* Entertainment
Home 94–97
Hospital 56
Hot Drinks 48
Hotel 81–82
House. *See* Home
  House Areas 94–97
Human Body 58–59
  Body Activities 60

I

Idioms 122–125
Immigration 66
Insects 109
Introducing Yourself 25
Invitations 28

J

Job Title 37

K

Kitchen 96

L

Landlord. *See* Estate Agent
Laundry 99
Legumes 52
Love 29–32
Loveless 32

M

Meals 47
Meat 47
  Meat Preparation 47
Media (News) 44–45
Misfortune 33
Money 72–73
  Banking 72
  Exchange Office 73
Months 112
Mountain Terms 85

N

Neighbours 98–99
Numbers 102–103
  Cardinal Numbers 103
  Ordinal Numbers 102

O

Outdoors 83–85

P

Paperwork 34
Payment 36
Police 65–67
Post 42–43
Preparations 50

Prepositions 80
Pronouns 132–133
  Demonstrative Pronouns 133
  Personal Pronouns 132
  Possessive Pronouns 133

Q

Questions 24

R

Relatives. *See* Family
Rent. *See* Estate Agent
Röschtigraben 12

S

Schriftdeutsch 8
Seafood 50
Seasons 112
Sexual Preferences 30
Shopping 52, 68–69
Slanguage 118–121
SMS 40–41
Snow Terms 84–85
Special Moments 33
Swiss Expressions 63
Swiss German 4–15
Swiss statistics 12–13

T

Telephone 38–39
Temperature 114–115
Time 110–113
  Measurements 110
  Moments in Time 111
  Telling Time 113
Time at Work 36
Toiletries 97

Toilets 104
Transportation 74–77
  Ticket Controllers 76
  Tickets 74–76
Travel 74–77
Typical Drinks 49

U

Use of High German 8–11
Use of Swiss German 12–14

V

Vegetables 52
Verbs 134–135
  Common Past Tenses 135
  Modal verbs 135
Vowels 19

W

Weather 114–115
Wedding Stuff 31
Work 34–37
Working Areas 36

Sali zämme - your Baseldütsch survival guide

About the authors

Sergio J. Lievano is a Swiss-Anglo-Colombian author brought up in the fresh surroundings of his family's 'Hacienda', a coffee plantation high up in the Andes.

Sergio is a qualified economist and worked in this field for more than 12 years in several countries. He also studied comics and illustration at the Joso Comic School in Barcelona where he developed his cartoonist talent. As he once said: "...Humour is the best medicine for a bad economy..". The Nobel Prize committee are still reviewing this major economic breakthrough principle.

In the meantime, Sergio is the author of five other books: four of them published in Switzerland and one in Colombia. Last year he wrote a worldwide best seller, unfortunately he forgot to save it...

Currently he is the illustrator and graphic designer for several Swiss companies, including ZVV, Syngenta and Marché Restaurant.

For more information visit
www.drawingelephants.ch

Sali zämme - your Baseldütsch survival guide

Nicole Egger was born and grew up in Zurich. She received her master's in linguistics and literature from the University of Zurich. During her studies and since her degree she has been teaching German and Swiss German to the increasingly international community in Switzerland.

She spent a year in Beijing learning Chinese which enables her to sympathise with newcomers to Switzerland who are confronted with a difficult, funny-sounding language. Since she has a strong interest in understanding the mechanisms of different languages and has also studied Latin, English, French, Spanish and Portuguese, she is perceptive to the difficulties that students may encounter. But her real challenge is to encourage people who are learning a foreign language to become confident and competent in a way that they can have fun doing it.

Translator

Walter Loeliger was born in Basel and grew up speaking Baseldütsch. After his studies he lived in the eastern part of Switzerland and in the Engadin for several years where he got to know and grew fond of other Swiss dialects. Since 1994 he is back in Basel. For many years he worked as a teacher. Today he creates and edits school books for Swiss schools. He strives to bring educational, creative and linguistic demands together.

Walter Loeliger is also a freelance writer and lyricist, using either High German or his home dialect, Baseldütsch. He writes satirical texts for performances before and during Basler Fasnacht, dealing in a critical as well as humoristic way with Basel and the world. He has a special ear for the peculiarities of Baseldütsch and cares about its preservation. He himself speaks a modern, unstilted Baseldütsch and enjoys the rich vocabulary of this region with all its charm.

Sali zämme - your Baseldütsch survival guide

Acknowledgements

A lot of people have helped in many ways to make this book a reality. They have given us their time and knowledge to help this book be amusing and useful. To all of them our sincere gratitude. In particular we would like to mention:

Anja Kauf, Dianne Dicks, Monica Vischer, Miguel Lievano, George Oswald, Markus and Anja Oswald, Thomas Oswald, Marché, and Werner Schaerer.

We thank BVB (Basler Verkehrs-Betriebe, the public transport corporation owned by Canton Basel-Stadt) for their support of this book.

Sali zämme - your Baseldütsch survival guide

About Bergli Books (the publisher...)

Bergli Books publishes books in English that focus on life in Switzerland and explore social and intercultural issues, history, culture, attitudes and values:

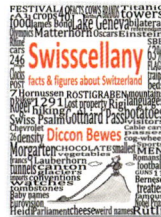

Swisscellany – facts & figures about Switzerland *compiled by Diccon Bewes and illustrated by Mischa Kammermann* is a treasure-trove of serious and not-so-serious lists. For example, you can learn how to play Hornussen, be able to sing along to the Swiss National Anthem and understand what the Geneva Conventions stand for.
ISBN 978-3-905252-24-8.

Going Local – your guide to Swiss schooling *by Margaret Oertig* is an authoritative guide for parents who wish to gain a better understanding of the Swiss school system. It maps out all the stages of schooling from kindergarten to university in all 26 cantons, providing key facts and the terminology needed in German, French and Italian.
ISBN 978-3-905252-25-5.

Cheese – slices of Swiss culture *by Sue Style, photographs by Nikos Kapelis* and historical documents and works of art from the Roth Foundation in Burgdorf. Meet the country's innovative cheese makers and discover the finest cheeses, cheese recipes and what to look for to treat your taste buds. ISBN 978-3-905252-20-0.

Swiss History in a Nutshell *by Grégoire Nappey, cartoons by Mix & Remix, translated by Robert Middleton.* Learn about the most fascinating moments in Switzerland's rich and colourful history. Cartoons (naughty and nice) illustrate this kaleidoscope of key events that have created Switzerland as it is today. ISBN 978-3-905252-19-4.

Swiss Cookies – biscuits for Christmas and all year round *by Andrew Rushton and Katalin Fekete*, a selection of the most famous and traditional Swiss cookies and bakes, with recipes and photographs from Betty Bossi. ISBN 978-3-905252-17-0.

Sali zämme - your Baseldütsch survival guide

At Home – a selection of stories *by Franz Hohler*, one of Switzerland's most popular writers and performers. This collection includes some of his most famous stories and sketches in English translation such as 'The End of the World' (Der Weltuntergang), 'Conditions for Taking Nourishment' (Bedingungen für die Nahrungsaufnahme), among others. ISBN 978-3-905252-18-7.

Ticking Along with Swiss Kids *by Dianne Dicks and Katalin Fekete, illustrations by Marc Locatelli*. A colourful and fun way for children from ages 6 to 12 to learn all they need to enjoy making friends and feeling at home. It explains Swiss languages, food, festivities, what kids read, sing, play and how they get along. Includes songs, maps, lists of places to visit and a 32-card language game and has hundreds of photographs and playful illustrations throughout. ISBN 978-3-905252-15-6.

Hoi – your Swiss German survival guide *by Sergio J. Lievano and Nicole Egger* (Swiss German / Zürich dialect – English edition of Sali zämme). ISBN 978-3-905252-13-2.

Hoi Zäme – Schweizerdeutsch leicht gemacht *von Sergio J. Lievano und Nicole Egger* macht mit seinen über 200 witzigen und farbenfrohen Cartoons das Erlernen der Sprache zu einem vergnüglichen Erlebnis. (*Hoi Zäme* is the Swiss German (Zurich dialect) – High German edition of Sali zämme) ISBN 978-3-905252-22-4.

Hoi et après... Manuel de survie en suisse allemand *by Sergio J. Lievano and Nicole Egger*. (Zürich dialect - French edition of Sali zämme). ISBN 978-3-905252-16-3.

Swiss Me *by Roger Bonner*, illustrations *by Edi Barth*. Humorous stories about life in Switzerland. ISBN 978-3-905252-11-8.

Culture Smart Switzerland *by Kendall Maycock*. A quick guide to customs, etiquette and history of Switzerland. ISBN 978-3-905252-12-5.

Beyond Chocolate – understanding Swiss culture *by Margaret Oertig-Davidson*, an in-depth discussion of the cultural attitudes and values of the Swiss, for newcomers and long-term residents. ISBN 978-3-905252-21-7.

Sali zämme - your Baseldütsch survival guide

Schokolade ist nicht alles – ein Leitfaden zur Schweizer Kultur *von Margaret Oertig-Davidson. Ein Führer durch die Schweizer Lebensart für jeden Neuankömmling und alle, die sich bereits als Insider fühlen. (German edition of Beyond Chocolate.)* ISBN 978-3-905252-10-1.

Lifting the Mask – your guide to Basel Fasnacht *by Peter Habicht, illustrations by Fredy Prack.* ISBN 978-3-905252-04-0.

pfyffe ruesse schränze – eine Einführung in die Basler Fasnacht *von Peter Habicht, Illustrationen von Fredy Prack. (German edition of Lifting the Mask.)* ISBN 978-3-905252-09-05.

Inside Outlandish *by Susan Tuttle, illustrated by ANNA, a collection of essays that takes you to the heart of feeling at home in strange, new places.* ISBN 978-3-9520002-8-1.

A Taste of Switzerland *by Sue Style, with over 50 recipes that show the richness of this country's diverse gastronomic cultures.* ISBN 978-3-9520002-7-4.

Cupid's Wild Arrows; intercultural romance and its consequences *edited by Dianne Dicks, contains personal experiences of 55 authors living with two worlds in one partnership.* ISBN 978-3-9520002-2-9.

Ticking Along Too *edited by Dianne Dicks, entertaining and informative personal experiences, a mix of social commentary, warm admiration and observations of the Swiss as friends, neighbours and business partners.* ISBN 978-3-9520002-1-2.

Ticking Along Free *edited by Dianne Dicks, with more stories about living with the Swiss, this time also with some prominent Swiss writers.* ISBN 978-3-905252-02-6.

www.bergli.ch

1. **Vogel Gryff:** Old traditional event in Kleinbasel, on the right side of the Rhine *(one day in January)*
2. **Basler Fasnacht:** Carneval in the city *(three days and nights in February or March)*
3. **Muba:** Swiss fair *(ten days in February or March)*
4. **Basel World:** World's most important fair for jewellery and watches *(ten days in spring)*
5. **Art Basel:** World famous art fair *(one week in June)*
6. **Bündelidaag:** Day after the last schoolday before the summerholidays *(end of June)*
7. **Basel Tattoo:** International tattoo show with pipes, drums and military bands *(10 days in July)*
8. **Erscht Auguscht:** Swiss national day with fireworks on the Rhine *(evening of July 31.)*
9. **Riischwimme:** Thousands swimming together down the Rhine *(evening in August)*
10. **Em Bebbi si Jazz:** Swing, Jazz and Dixieland in one part of the old town *(one evening in August)*
11. **Herbschtmäss:** Traditional fair at different places in town *(two weeks end of October)*
12. **Wienachtsmäärt:** Christmas fair at different places in town *(three weeks in December)*